# ROAD RACERS

# &

# THEIR TRAINING

*edited by Joe Henderson*

First published in 1995 by Tafnews Press,
Book Division of Track & Field News,
2570 El Camino Real, Suite 606,
Mountain View, CA 94040 USA.

Standard Book Number 0-911521-44-5

Printed in the United States of America


Cover design and production: Teresa Tam


Photo credits:
Cover by Richard Lee Slotkin
Title page by DUOMO/Steven E. Sutton

Dedicated to

FRED WILT

who first taught us how runners train.

# CONTENTS

STARTING LINES .................................................................7

MARK ALLEN .................................................................12
GABRIELE ANDERSEN .....................................................14
RUTH ANDERSON ...........................................................16
TOM ANSBERRY ..............................................................18
GORDON BAKOULIS ........................................................20
ARTURO BARRIOS ...........................................................22
KEITH BRANTLY ..............................................................24
AMBY BURFOOT .............................................................26
DIANE BUSSA .................................................................28
DEREK CLAYTON .............................................................30
MARK CONOVER .............................................................32
MARK COOGAN ..............................................................34
TED CORBITT ..................................................................36
    GRANDPA TED ...........................................................38
MARK COVERT ...............................................................41
NAN DOAK-DAVIS ..........................................................43
MISTI DEMKO .................................................................45
PATTI DILLON .................................................................47
    THE NEW PATTI .........................................................49
NANCY DITZ ...................................................................51
JEROME DRAYTON ..........................................................53
JANICE ETTLE ..................................................................56
GARY FANELLI .................................................................58
BARBARA FILUTZE ...........................................................60
TOM FLEMING ................................................................62
JACK FOSTER ...................................................................64
NORM FRANK .................................................................66
JEFF GALLOWAY ..............................................................68
    JEFF OF ALL TRADES ...................................................70
JACQUELINE GAREAU ......................................................73

TIM GARGIULO ..................................................................75
MIKI GORMAN ..................................................................77
NORM GREEN ....................................................................79
JIM HAGE .............................................................................81
JACQUELINE HANSEN ....................................................83
DAN HELD ..........................................................................85
HAL HIGDON ....................................................................87
RON HILL ............................................................................89
SISTER MARION IRVINE ................................................91
    NUN BETTER ...............................................................93
JULIE ISPHORDING .........................................................96
JEFF JACOBS ......................................................................98
DON JANICKI ..................................................................100
LYNN JENNINGS ............................................................102
    LOOKING UP TO LYNN ...........................................104
DON KARDONG ..............................................................107
JOHN A. KELLEY .............................................................109
JOHN J. KELLEY ..............................................................111
    THE YOUNGER KELLEY ..........................................113
JOHN KESTON ..................................................................115
SANDY KIDDY ..................................................................117
JANIS KLECKER ................................................................119
INGRID KRISTIANSEN ....................................................121
DOUG KURTIS ..................................................................123
ANNE MARIE LAUCK .....................................................125
JERRY LAWSON ................................................................127
JOE LeMAY .........................................................................129
PETER MAHER ...................................................................131
SHIRLEY MATSON ...........................................................133
GREG MEYER .....................................................................135
LORRAINE MOLLER ........................................................137
KENNY MOORE .................................................................139
MARK NENOW ...................................................................141
JOAN NESBIT .....................................................................143
    ARRIVING LATE ..........................................................145
PETE PFITZINGER ............................................................147

STEVE PLASENCIA ...... 149
LISA RAINSBERGER ...... 151
SUZANNE RAY ...... 153
PAUL REESE ...... 155
BILL RODGERS ...... 157
    RODGERS RETIRED? ...... 159
BOB SCHLAU ...... 161
FRANK SHORTER ...... 163
    AMONG FRIENDS ...... 165
TAMMY SLUSSER ...... 168
JOY SMITH ...... 170
KEN SPARKS ...... 172
JUDI ST. HILAIRE ...... 174
KATHRINE SWITZER ...... 176
STEVE TAYLOR ...... 178
ANN TRASON ...... 180
    RACIN' TRASON ...... 182
JOHN TREACY ...... 184
MARIA TRUJILLO ...... 186
JOHN TUTTLE ...... 188
JOAN ULLYOT ...... 190
PRISCILLA WELCH ...... 192
JANE WELZEL ...... 194
JEANNIE WOKASCH ...... 196

FINISH LINES ...... 198

# Starting Lines

---

FRED WILT was one of the most important coaches this country has ever known. His work pulled American distance runners out of the Dark Ages.

As a runner who finished 11th and 21st in his Olympic 10,000s, he set out to learn what the world's best runners knew and his countrymen didn't. This research grew into a 1959 book, *How They Train*, which literally reproduced dozens of training programs.

Hal Higdon, then a young writer-artist, illustrated that book. "It was the archetypical training book of all time," says Higdon. "Talk to any distance runner from the 1960s, and most likely he read *How They Train* and was influenced by it."

The Golden Age of U.S. running began soon afterward. Jim Beatty, Max Truex, Buddy Edelen, Billy Mills, Bob Schul, Bill Dellinger, Jim Ryun, Gerry Lindgren suddenly raced among the world's best.

Higdon adds, "I don't know if we can relate the success that Americans began to have in distance events in the '60s entirely to the book's wide distribution. But it certainly had an effect."

When Wilt died in 1994 at age 73, I paid tribute to him in the newsletter *Running Commentary*. A reader named Rich Englehart then wrote to praise Wilt as the creator of training-profile books.

"In my concept of heaven," said Englehart, "the training diaries of every runner who ever lived are on file. Naturally, the how-they-train books are my all-time favorites.

"So I'm sorry to see Fred Wilt gone. He established the genre, and as long as he was alive there was always the chance that he'd write another one. Now the whole concept seems to be disappearing."

Englehart added that "there are loads of articles and books that describe ideal training programs. But the how-they-train profiles show you what runners actually DO. It's like the difference between a philosopher's view of how we SHOULD live compared to an historian's or a sociologist's descriptions of how they do live."

In 1970, I had training collected profiles for a book with the same title as this one, *Road Racers & Their Training*. "If you ever get the urge to do another," said Englehart, "I'll buy it."

Nice that someone remembers a book from so long ago that came and went so quickly, I thought. But the book he suggested wouldn't have gotten a second thought if Ed Fox hadn't seen that letter.

Fox is the publisher of *Track & Field News*. T&FN had issued *How They Train* and *Road Racers*, among many other training-profile books.

Fox's response contained the quickest offer ever. He clipped Englehart's letter, circled the I'll-buy-it paragraph in red, wrote in the margin, "We'd publish it, " and mailed me this note without further comment.

Within days, we had a deal for *Road Racers II*. Within weeks, I began looking for runners to fill it.

QUESTIONNAIRES WENT OUT to more than 100 of them. The book would almost write itself, if enough candidates responded in the detail requested. I had little more to do than edit their answers—if they bothered to answer.

IF. . . That was my worry. Twenty-five years ago, I had no such doubt. I was closer to the top runners then, but the distance between us has grown.

They were my agemates then, not a generation removed as most of today's race leaders are. The earlier leaders were minutes ahead of me, not miles. They were hungry for attention from writers like me, not hounded by the media.

Today's top runners are both more visible and harder to find. They either don't share addresses and phone numbers, or are never home. Layers of coaches and agents guard their privacy, and often speak for them.

These runners are pros. They might ask for interview fees that I couldn't pay.

Or so I feared. The concern lasted only a week, until the first return envelope arrived.

It came from world champion Lynn Jennings, no less. She took time to answer every question and to pen a great line: "I am not an overmileage fanatic, and I am not an overracing geek."

Dozens of athletes replied after Jennings. All took similar care, and many added personal notes of thanks for including them.

Joan Nesbit apologized for being "sloppy," and said "this is a busy time for me." She wrote this right after placing third at the World Indoors and sixth at the World Cross Country Championships, and while coaching a college team in midseason.

I wish you could see the questionnaires themselves. Reading them in the runner's own handwriting—crossouts and all—introduced me to the real people behind the incredible performances.

Much of this feeling survived the editing and translation into print. After reading these profiles, you too will feel closer to these runners—if only on paper.

I sensed an eagerness to tell their stories in their own words. *Road Racers II* is more their book than mine.

**FOUR OLYMPIC MEDALISTS,** plus another from the World Championships, appear here. So do 11 current or former world record holders (and many more in their age groups), along with more than two dozen Olympians and a dozen winners of the Boston and New York City Marathons.

Yet this isn't a who's-who of road racing. For a more complete volume of biographies, I direct you to the *Road Race Management Guide to Prize Money Races and Elite Athletes*. (Available from RRM, 4904 Glen Cove Parkway, Bethesda, MD 20816.)

*Road Racers* gives closer looks at fewer runners. They represent a cross-section of the sport—men and women, young and old, active and legendary, road specialists and running generalists.

Some appear strictly for their running, while others are better known now for writing or coaching. Their ages range from the mid-20s to the late 80s.

For practical reasons, I selected mostly English-speakers who live in the United States and Canada. They were easiest to locate and communicate with, and their backgrounds are most like the readers'. You're likely to see some of them at your own races.

Everyone in the book wanted to be here. No one was prodded—or paid—to contribute. These runners recognize that you look up to them and support their efforts. They volunteered to share their hard-won lessons with you.

As editor, my first impulse was to separate these 80 runners into categories—men and women, open and masters, foreign and domestic, short and long distances, present and past stars. Then I remembered: Road racing isn't like that.

All types of runners blend together at races. We all use the same starting line, and run at the same time (if not at the same pace) toward a common finish line.

This book reflects that blend. The runners all line up together here, alphabetically.

THE PROFILES follow a standard format: introductory paragraph, biographical data, best times, overall training plan, sample week and favorite workout.

Keep in mind as you read their stories that the facts date from summer 1995 and might have changed in the meantime. These profiles are snapshots taken at one time in the runners' life stories that are always undergoing examination and revision.

Note, too, that the runners chose which period they wanted to emphasize. Some went for the training leading up to their best races, while others focused on what they do now. Some picked actual workouts, others an idealized program.

Descriptions of workouts vary widely, both in amount of detail and in wording. For instance, they call short bursts of speed "pickups," strides," "striders" and "strideouts." They call the end-of-workout time either a "warmdown" or a "cooldown." They call the spaces between repeats "recovery," "jog," "interval" or "rest."

These runners generally list their road runs in miles but their track workouts in meters. They refer to interval training in shorthand such as "10 x 400," meaning 400 meters repeated 10 times. I've left the wording as they listed it.

**THE ROAD RACERS THEMSELVES** wrote most of this book. My biggest job was chasing them down.

Helping to locate multiple runners were the *Road Race Management Guide* (see address above), Marty Post at *Runner's World*, Ryan Lamppa at the Road Running Information Center and Jack Fleming at the Boston AA Marathon.

Several agents linked me to their athletes: Glenn Latimer, C.J. Olivares, Don Paul and Luis Posso.

These friends of mine put me in touch with friends of theirs: Carl Andersen, Hal Higdon, Ken Lee, Laurie McCann, Tom Sturak, Mike Tymn and Katherine Williams.

Thanks to all!

Joe Henderson
Eugene, Oregon
September 1995

# MARK ALLEN

> You know him as a triathlete—possibly the world's greatest all-round endurance athlete. Between 1989 and '93, he won every Hawaiian Ironman and set the record for this ultradistance triathlon. For our purposes, Allen is also the finest RUNNER in his sport. He has broken 30 minutes in the 10-K—while spending only about a third of his training time running. The mix of sports has helped keep him free of serious injuries throughout his career.

## ❏ MARK ALLEN

Cardiff, California. Born January 12th, 1958, in California. 6'0", 160 pounds. Married. Occupation: triathlete. Began racing in 1980. Runs for Nike. Self-coached.

## ❏ BEST TIMES

5-K, 14:37; 10-K, 29:59; marathon, 2:40:04 (in Ironman); Ironman triathlon, 8:07:45.

## ❏ TRAINING PLAN

Bulk of training is aerobic, only a small percentage anaerobic. Strength training is also important. The yearly pattern: three months of winter base work; 10 weeks of speed; another short block of aerobic training in July; eight weeks of overdistance plus speed for Hawaiian Ironman.

## ❏ SAMPLE WEEK

Including 60 to 65 miles of running during pre-Ironman period.

Sunday—two-hour run, easy 4-K swim.

Monday—4-K swim, 50-mile bike, 15-K run.

Tuesday—20-K fartlek run, 4-K swim, 40-K bike.

Wednesday—200-K bike, five-mile run, easy swim.

Thursday—40-mile easy bike, 5-K swim, 15-K run.

Friday—5-K of running intervals on track, 10 miles of intervals or time trial on bike, 3-K swim.

Saturday—100-mile bike, five-mile run.

❏ FAVORITE WORKOUT

Fartlek for run, since it is closest to race effort.

# GABRIELE ANDERSEN

*She didn't die after her memorable struggle to the finish in the 1984 Olympic Marathon. She didn't even suffer serious after-effects, other than the burden of unsought fame that incident brought her. She didn't fade out of the sport. Andersen, a dual Swiss-U.S. citizen, did some of her best running AFTER Los Angeles—including a 1:15 half-marathon at age 40. She continuously held Switzerland's national marathon record from 1983 to '94.*

## ❏ GABRIELE ANDERSEN

Sun Valley, Idaho. Born March 20th, 1945, in Thun, Switzerland. 5'4", 113 pounds. Married. Occupation: ski instructor, concierge. Began racing in 1972. Coached by Bob Sevene and self.

## ❏ BEST TIMES

5-K, 16:30 (1985 & '88); 10-K, 33:20 (1983); half-marathon, 1:15 (1985); marathon, 2:33 (1983).

## ❏ TRAINING PLAN

I used the winter for buildup, longer distances, slower pace, hill work, some weight work. In summer, I ran faster shorter intervals. I cross-trained with swimming, cross-country skiing and some cycling.

## ❏ SAMPLE WEEK

Before a marathon, totaling 90 to 100 miles, all at 6000 feet elevation.

Sunday—A.M., 20 miles; P.M., easy 30-minute swim.

Monday—A.M., eight miles easy. P.M., 5-6 miles easy.

Tuesday—A.M., 14-16 x 400; two-mile warmup and cooldown. P.M., 4-5 miles easy or swim.

Wednesday—A.M., 8-10 miles. P.M., 5-6 miles.

Thursday--A.M., 3-4-mile tempo run or 4-5 miles of repeats on track. P.M., 4-5 miles easy.

Friday—A.M., 8-10 miles. P.M., 4-5 miles or swim.

Saturday—eight miles easy or hike.

❏ FAVORITE WORKOUT

On the road, 12-18 x 350-400 yards (I count steps) every two minutes, which gives me about 40 seconds rest-jogging between repeats. There is no pressure of times, but it is still a hard workout.

# Ruth Anderson

*She flat-out loves to race—any distance, any surface, anytime. Within two months in 1978, Anderson set PRs ranging from one mile to 100 miles. This love affair has lasted ever since she discovered racing at age 44. Both a pioneer in and promoter of masters running, she has competed in all 11 World Veterans Championships. The meet honored her as its final torchbearer in 1995.*

## ❏ RUTH P. ANDERSON

Oakland, California. Born July 27th, 1929, in Omaha, Nebraska. 5'8", 125 pounds. Married, one child. Occupation: retired nuclear chemist. Began racing in 1973. Runs for Bay Area Ultrarunners. Self-coached.

## ❏ BEST TIMES

Mile, 5:57 (1978); 5-K, 19:37 (1978); 10-K, 39:57 (1977); 15-K, 1:01:14 (1978); 20-K, 1:25:49 (1976); half-marathon, 1:29:33 (1978); 25-K, 1:44:12 (1977); 30-K, 2:11:40 (1979); 20 miles, 2:21:13 (1977); marathon, 3:04:19 (1978); 50-K, 4:09:09 (1980); 50 miles, 7:10:58 (1980); 100-K, 9:57:30 (1978); 12 hours, 63.1 miles (1987); 100 miles, 16:50:47 (1978); 24 hours, 110.25 miles (1986).

## ❏ TRAINING PLAN

My training is geared to a goal—a major event or series of events. 1977 and '78 were my best record years at many distances, with the marathon always the main focus. Racing often was used for speedwork, except before a track meet, when intervals were included. Cross country training helped all off-road racing. I used all these elements nearly year-round.

## ❏ SAMPLE WEEK

No one week was ever "typical," especially with racing every weekend. This was an actual week during my best racing period of summer 1978, when the week's mileage of 40 was less then my usual 50-55.

Monday—hilly five miles in 39:18.

Tuesday—trail 15-K with a group.

Wednesday—9.8 miles with colleagues from work.

Thursday—4.5 miles after flying to Portland, Oregon.

Friday—hilly five miles at race pace on Cascade Runoff course.

Saturday—2.5 miles on Cascade course with daughter, near race pace.

Sunday—Cascade Runoff 15-K in PR of 1:01:14.

## ❏ FAVORITE WORKOUT

The Tuesday night runs in the summer are on soft surfaces (fire roads and trails), have steep hills or gradual inclines for fartlek-type speedwork and strengthening, and I always have good support and advice from fellow runners.

# TOM ANSBERRY

*Okay, it's a stretch to call him a "road racer." Like many younger, faster athletes, Ansberry's main ambitions still point him toward the track. There he won the 1994 national title in the 10,000 and qualified for the World Championships in '95. But—like his coach Alberto Salazar before him—Ansberry can shift smoothly to the roads. There he also won a '94 national title in the 10-K and PRed in the half-marathon that year.*

## ❑ THOMAS HENRY ANSBERRY, JR.

Portland, Oregon. Born August 22nd, 1963, in Okinawa. 5'10", 138 pounds. Married, two children. Occupation: salesman. Began racing in 1975. Runs for Nike. Coach: Alberto Salazar.

## ❑ BEST TIMES

5000, 13:38 (1992); 10,000, 28:03 (1995); half-marathon, 1:02:50 (1994); marathon, 2:19:01 (1995).

## ❑ TRAINING PLAN

I try to maintain an overall strength base throughout the year (with high mileage, over hilly terrain). Depending on the race or season that I am preparing for, I add appropriate work (speed, tempo runs, long runs, etc.).

## ❑ SAMPLE WEEK

Of 75-80 miles.

Sunday—10 miles.

Monday—A.M., five miles. P.M., 10 miles hilly (pressing over hills).

Tom Ansberry (No. 101) leads the pack at the 1994 Goodwill Games.

Tuesday—A.M., five miles easy. P.M., 10 miles easy.

Wednesday—A.M., five miles easy. P.M., track workout of 4 x 800/300 in 2:12/46 seconds—comfortable, under control; 20-minute warmup and cooldown.

Thursday—A.M., travel. P.M., 20 minutes easy.

Friday—A.M., 20 minutes easy. P.M., 20 minutes easy.

Saturday—A.M., 20 minutes. P.M., race 10,000.

## ❏ FAVORITE WORKOUT

Six times one mile. There is nothing fun about it, but it is a good indicator of 10-K race fitness.

# GORDON BAKOULIS

*Though still young herself, Bakoulis is a throwback to an era of women's long-distance running when a woman could begin as a "jogger" and still graduate to high levels of the sport. This doesn't happen much anymore, now that youth programs hone runners' skills early. Bakoulis, however, skipped high school and college track and cross country. She began as an exercise-runner, then eased into "recreational" races. Only at 24 did she get competitive. At 30, she made the U.S. World Championships marathon team.*

## ❏ M. GORDON BAKOULIS

New York City. Born February 14th, 1961, in Princeton, New Jersey. 5'6½", 108 pounds. Single. Occupation: magazine editor. Began racing in 1985. Runs for Moving Comfort. Coach: Benji Durden.

## ❏ BEST TIMES

3000, 9:18 (1992); 5000, 16:01 (1992); four miles, 21:09 (1989); 8-K, 23:26 (1990); 10-K, 32:45 (1992); 10 miles, 55:07 (1991); 20-K, 1:09:14 (1992); half-marathon, 1:11:34 (1992); marathon, 2:33:01 (1989).

## ❏ TRAINING PLAN

I emphasize three areas: (1) balance—fitting in the elements of long run, speedwork, cross-training, weights and rest; (2) flexibility—I work fulltime, train outdoors and have to think about safety, so my schedule can't be set in stone; (3) listening to my body.

## ❏ SAMPLE WEEK

This is what I actually did about five weeks before a marathon. Mileage totaled 90.

Sunday—A.M., three-mile warmup; three miles of "ins and outs" (jog curves, sprint straights) on track. P.M., one hour and 25 minutes easy while watching a race.

Monday—A.M., 56-minute (7.5-mile) easy, flat run; felt good. P.M., five-mile bike (warmup), weights at health club.

Tuesday—A.M., 35-minutes (five-mile) run to work, light pick-ups. P.M., two-mile warmup; 2 x 300, 2 x 600, 2 x 800 (400 recovery); 4.5-mile cooldown.

Wednesday—A.M., 4.5-mile easy run to work. P.M., 6.5 miles easy; weights at health club.

Thursday—A.M., two-mile easy run to work. P.M., 4.5-mile warmup; 6.5-mile fartlek run (with group), including 4 x 400; 1.5-mile cooldown; felt good.

Friday—A.M., 6.5 miles easy (very!) in 47 minutes; felt sore. P.M., weights at health club.

Saturday—2:33 run (21 miles); windy but felt strong.

❏ **FAVORITE WORKOUT**

10-K on the track with 800 hard/200 recovery, repeated 10 times, with no break in running (except if needed for water at 5-K). It tells me I'm ready for a half-marathon or marathon.

# ARTURO BARRIOS

> *Apart from the running, his is a great American success story: came to the U.S. from Mexico, studied engineering at Texas A&M University, remained in this country, married, became a citizen, fathered twins. Running, of course, started Barrios in these directions. It took him to world track records in the 10,000, 20,000 and one-hour run. He's the only person ever to run a half-marathon in less than an hour on the track. He'll probably complete his career on the roads, where he is a 2:08 marathoner.*

## ❏ ARTURO BARRIOS

Boulder, Colorado. Born December 12th, 1962, in Mexico City. 5'10", 133 pounds. Married, two children. Occupation: athlete. Began racing in 1978. Runs for Reebok. Coach: Tadeusz Kepka.

## ❏ BEST TIMES

Track: 1500, 3:37.61 (1989); 3000, 7:35.71 (1989); 5000, 13:07.70 (1989); 10,000, 27:08.23 (1989); 20,000, 56:55.4 (1991); one hour, 21,101 meters/13.11 miles (1991). Road: four miles, 17:43 (1986); 10-K, 27:41 (1986); 15-K, 42:35 (1986); half-marathon, 1:00:41 (1991); marathon, 2:08:28 (1994).

## ❏ TRAINING PLAN

In addition to running workouts, I do lots of stretching, adequate warmup, weight lifting for upper body (mild work for legs), adequate cooldown.

## ❏ SAMPLE WEEK

Of 100 to 105 miles.

Sunday—easy day, six miles plus 10 x 100 strides.

**Arturo Barrios**

Monday—A.M., 10 miles. P.M., six miles.

Tuesday—A.M., 10 x 1000 on track. P.M., six miles.

Wednesday—A.M., 10 miles with last mile of fartlek. P.M., six miles.

Thursday—A.M., four-mile hill workout. P.M., six miles.

Friday—A.M., 20 x 400 on track. P.M., six miles.

Saturday—long run, 12-13 miles for 10-K or 18-20 miles for marathon.

## ❏ FAVORITE WORKOUT

10 x 1000 meters in 2:45-2:47, with last two in 2:42 and 2:38. It gives me a lot of confidence going into a race.

# KEITH BRANTLY

*This is the right way to progress: from short distances to long, by well-calculated steps. Brantly took these steps deliberately, focusing on building speed for the track and short road races through his teens and 20s. He placed fourth in the 1988 Olympic 5000 trial. Brantly didn't really become a marathoner until almost 30, but by then was ready to take on any American. He was Olympic alternate in 1992 and won his first marathon three years later at 32.*

## ❏ KEITH BRANTLY

Fort Lauderdale, Florida. Born May 23rd, 1962, at Scott Air Force Base, Illinois. 5'10", 138 pounds. Married, one child. Occupation: athlete. Began racing in 1977. Runs for New Balance. Coach: David Martin.

## ❏ BEST TIMES

5000, 13:36; track 10,000, 28:10; road 10-K, 28:02; half-marathon, 1:01:30; marathon, 2:12:49.

## ❏ TRAINING PLAN

Avoiding injury is paramount. I train in a four-week block of weeks with ascending mileage and difficulty until the fourth week, which is a very light week with possibly a race.

## ❏ SAMPLE WEEK

Of 142 miles.

Sunday—25 miles at 6:10-6:40 pace on hills.

Monday—A.M., 12 miles on grass, steady. P.M., seven miles

**Keith Brantly at the 1992
Olympic Trials marathon.**

easy; strides.

Tuesday—A.M., eight miles easy. P.M., three-mile warmup, 2 x 5-mile tempo runs at 5:00 pace with three-minute jog between; two-mile warmdown; weights.

Wednesday—A.M., 10 miles easy. P.M., five miles easy; strides.

Thursday—A.M., eight miles steady. P.M., 12 miles easy; strides.

Friday—A.M., 10 miles easy. P.M., two-mile warmup; 3 x 3200 in 9:00-9:10 with three-minute jog between; two-mile warmdown.

Saturday—12 miles steady.

## ❏ FAVORITE WORKOUT

Warm up two miles; 1600, 1200, 800, 800, 400, 400, 800, 800, 1200, 1600 with one-minute jog recovery between each; warm down two miles. This workout teaches pace control and has all the elements.

# AMBY BURFOOT

Lots of runners get credit for turning U.S. long-distance racing around a generation ago. Most commonly, you hear the names Frank Shorter and Bill Rodgers for all they did in the 1970s. But this country's long Boston Marathon drought really ended in 1968, when Burfoot became the first American to win there in 11 years. Later, he came within ONE SECOND of Buddy Edelen's long-standing national marathon record. Amby went on to serve as editor of Runner's World magazine.

## ❏ AMBROSE JOEL BURFOOT

Emmaus, Pennsylvania. Born August 19th, 1946, in Charlottesville, Virginia. 6'0", 140 pounds. Married, two children. Occupation: editor. Began racing in 1963. Runs for Lehigh Valley Road Runners. Self-coached.

## ❏ BEST TIMES

Mile, 4:19.8; two miles, 8:44; three miles, 13:44; six miles, 29:26; marathon, 2:14:29.

## ❏ TRAINING PLAN

The elements: (1) long run, very slow, 60 to 120 minutes; now trying some run-walk (four-minute runs, one-minute walks); (2) tempo runs, nine minutes at 10-K race pace; (3) max-VO$_2$ repeats, three minutes at slightly under 5-K race pace; (4) speed intervals, 30 seconds. In fact, one of my precepts is "multiples of three." That is, I do intervals of 30 seconds for speed and efficiency, three minutes for max VO$_2$, and nine minutes for tempo.

**This was Amby Burfoot after his 1968 Boston victory.**

## ❏ SAMPLE WEEK

I trained best when I trained most consistently and methodi-
cally—often the same workouts day after day and week after
week. Say, six miles easy in the morning, eight to 10 easy in
the afternoon. At peak, I did intervals of 200 to 800 at fast but
controlled pace twice a week.

## ❏ FAVORITE WORKOUT

I always liked 200s a lot—felt they made me quicker and more
efficient. I always did best with max-$VO_2$ workouts—800s
(four to eight) at 5-K race pace or slightly under.

# DIANE BUSSA

*You name it, Bussa has seen it—and in most cases done it. She has lived the history of women's running. She first raced as an nine-year-old, long before females enjoyed full running rights and opportunities. She ran as an age-grouper, high schooler and collegian. She competed with the nation's best in track and cross country, but now finds greatest success on the roads. Her times there range from a sub-33-minute 10-K to a 2:35 marathon.*

## ❏ DIANE BUSSA

Boulder, Colorado. Born August 9th, 1961, in Norfolk, Virginia. 5'3", 97 pounds. Single. Occupation: athlete and database administrator. Began racing in 1970. Runs for Moving Comfort. Coach: Dr. Jack Daniels.

## ❏ BEST TIMES

10-K, 32:41; 15-K, 49:34; 10 miles, 52:18; half-marathon, 1:11:48; 25-K, 1:25:34; marathon, 2:35:35.

## ❏ TRAINING PLAN

Run 70 to 80 miles per week (I can't do more mileage due to fulltime job), with emphasis on tempo running and speedwork. At least two recovery days between hard efforts.

## ❏ SAMPLE WEEK

Of 70 to 80 miles.

Sunday—two easy runs, 30-40 minutes each.

Monday—A.M., tempo work (e.g., 2-3 x 2 miles at 5:40-5:45 pace), followed by 10 miles moderate on the roads. P.M.,

30 minutes easy.

Tuesday—two easy runs.

Wednesday—two easy runs.

Thursday—A.M., some kind of speedwork (such as 3 x 1000, 6 x 200, 2 x 800). P.M., 30 minutes easy.

Friday—two easy runs.

Saturday—two easy runs.

## ❏ FAVORITE WORKOUT

Monday's workout above gives me strength and speed, as well as confidence.

# DEREK CLAYTON

*His is a name from the past, the now-distant past when the marathon enjoyed none of its present amenities. In the 1960s, this was a cult event whose practitioners were few. Yet times have progressed surprisingly little since Clayton's years. He was the first runner to break 2:10 (in 1967) and 2:09 (in '69), and not until 1981 did anyone run faster. Today, Clayton is back in Australia after long residence in the U.S. He competes internationally in bike-run duathlons.*

## ❑ DEREK CLAYTON

Beaumaris, Australia. Born November 17th, 1942, in England. 6'2", 160 pounds. Married, two children. Occupation: company director. Began racing in 1962. Runs for St. Stephens Harriers. Self-coached.

## ❑ BEST TIMES

1500, 3:47.8; mile, 4:07.5; 5000, 13:45.6; 10,000, 28:32.2; 10 miles, 47:38.1; 15 miles, 1:11:37; marathon, 2:08:33.

## ❑ TRAINING PLAN

Train hard (i.e., quality). Get plenty of rest/sleep. Eat well, a diet high in carbohydrates. Stretch daily. Get a weekly massage.

## ❑ SAMPLE WEEK

This was a typical week shortly before my 2:08:33 marathon, with mileage of 153.

Sunday—A.M., 17 miles in hills, solid. P.M., eight miles hard over flat course.

Monday—A.M., seven miles. P.M., 15 miles, last seven hard.

Tuesday—A.M., seven miles. P.M., 10 miles hard.

Wednesday—A.M., seven miles. P.M., 17 miles solid.

Thursday—A.M., seven miles. P.M., 15 miles over hilly course, hard.

Friday—A.M., seven miles. P.M., 12 miles easy.

Saturday—24 miles in approximately 2:20.

❑ FAVORITE WORKOUT

The 24-miler on Saturdays. I hated it because it was so tough, especially on top of a hard week. But it was valuable preparation for a fast marathon, and in my opinion still is.

# MARK CONOVER

His best victory didn't come in the 1988 Olympic Marathon Trial. Conover's biggest test began four years later, when the first symptoms of Hodgkin's Disease surfaced. Chemotherapy for this lymphatic cancer didn't end until mid-1994, but it resulted in his greatest triumph. Conover certified his return to health, after more than two years away from competition, by qualifying for the 1996 Marathon Trial.

## ❏ MARK ROBERT CONOVER

San Luis Obispo, California. Born May 28th, 1960, in Walnut Creek, California. 5'10", 140 pounds. Single. Occupation: magazine editor. Began racing in 1975. Runs for Brooks. Coach: James D. Hunt.

## ❏ BEST TIMES

1500, 3:56.8 (1981); 5000, 14:04 (1986); 8-K, 23:08 (1991); 10,000 track, 28:30.3 (1986); 10-K road, 28:36 (1988); 15-K, 44:16; 10 miles, 47:35 (1991); 30-K, 1:34:08 (1987); marathon, 2:12:26 (1988).

## ❏ TRAINING PLAN

Marathon fitness is gained by developing the lactate/anaerobic threshold, thus training focuses on that. Then, as fitness progresses, work is done to improve $VO_2$ max, which shouldn't be done to excess since short interval work at 5-K pace is very taxing when thrown into the mix of marathon training.

## ❏ SAMPLE WEEK

This is what I did in a 90-mile week prior to winning the 1988 Olympic Marathon Trial.

Sunday—20 miles at 6:00 pace.

Monday—A.M., four miles easy. P.M., seven miles at 5:45 pace.

Tuesday—A.M., four miles. P.M., two-mile warmup; mile in 4:38, jog 800, two-mile in 9:16, jog 800, mile in 4:36, jog 400, mile in 4:34; two-mile cooldown.

Wednesday—A.M., four miles. P.M., seven miles at 5:45 pace.

Thursday—A.M., four miles. P.M., two-mile warmup; 4 x 1000 in 2:45 with 400 jog between; two-mile cooldown.

Friday—A.M., four miles. P.M., seven miles at 5:45 pace.

Saturday—A.M., four miles. P.M., seven miles at 5:45 pace.

## ❏ FAVORITE WORKOUT

The Tuesday workout above, because it stresses the lactate-threshold pace. If done comfortably two days after the long run, it indicates the recovery process is going well.

# MARK COOGAN

*He was long typecast as a trackman and cross country runner when he jumped into the 1994 Boston Marathon. Coogan debuted with 2:13 at Boston to qualify for the next year's Pan-Am Games, where he was the silver medalist. The endurance work improved his track results. He made the '95 World Championships team in the 5000. "One of my problems," he said then, "is I am a jack of all trades in running but a master of none. I just love to race at different distances. I'm sure my PRs would be faster if I would focus better. I try to do too much." What would Coogan most like to do? "Win the Boston Marathon. I think I'd rather win Boston than the Olympics, because Boston has better fields and more tradition. The Olympic people couldn't care less about the athletes."*

## ❏ MARK J. COOGAN

Boulder, Colorado. Born May 1st, 1966, in Manhassett, New York. 5'10", 135 pounds. Married to Olympian Gwyn Coogan, one child. Occupation: runner. Began competing in 1982, first road race in 1988. Runs for New Balance. Coaches: Charles Torpey and Tadeusz Kepka.

## ❏ BEST TIMES

800, 1:51 (1991); mile, 3:58 (1992); 3000, 7:54 (1992); steeple, 8:26 (1992); 5000, 13:23 (1995); 10,000, 28:23 (1992); marathon, 2:13:24 (1994).

## ❏ TRAINING PLAN

Fall: Time to start building a base. Lots of longer runs (10 to 12 miles). Maybe do a road race or two, but never focus on them. Run the National Cross Country just off my natural strength and speed.

Winter: Start doing longer intervals, but keep distance up. Do an occasional indoor race or road race. Often run World Cross Country, but this winter I did Pan-Am Games.

Spring: Cut back on distance. Do more track workouts at a higher intensity. Race on the track, any distance from 1500 meters to 10-K.

Summer: Race till I'm dead, then take a rest until I feel like running once more.

## ❏ SAMPLE WEEK
Of 85 to 110 miles.

Sunday—16 miles at 6:00 pace, often last three miles at 5:30 pace.

Monday—A.M., 10 miles at 5:45 to 6:00 pace, 10 x 100-meter strides after. P.M., 8-K to 10-K with 10 x 100.

Tuesday—A.M., 5 x 2-K in 5:50 to 6:00, 10 x 100. P.M., 4 or 5 miles.

Wednesday—A.M., 20-K steady run. P.M., 10-K plus 10 x 100m.

Thursday—A.M., 4-K, then 10 x 200 hill. P.M., 8-K easy.

Friday—A.M., three sets of 5 x 400, 65 seconds for first four, then one in 62. P.M., 8-K to 10-K easy plus 10 x 100.

Saturday—10-K easy.

## ❏ FAVORITE WORKOUT
4 x 2-K in 5:45. Doing this at Boulder tells me I can run with the best of them (including Kenyans, Mexicans, whoever).

# TED CORBITT

*Of all the foundation-layers for running's glory years, none did more good work than Corbitt: Olympic marathoner, record-setting ultrarunner, RRCA co-founder, pioneering course-certifier. His story appears in the accompanying sidebar.*

## ❏ THEODORE CORBITT

New York City. Born January 31st, 1919, in Dunbarton, South Carolina. 5'9¼", 134 pounds. Widower, one child. Occupation: physical therapist. Began racing in 1933. Ran for New York Pioneer Club. Coaches: Joe Yancey, Dr. William Ruthrauff, Percy Cerutty.

## ❏ BEST TIMES

Mile, 4:27; marathon, 2:26:44 (1958); 50 miles, 5:34:01 (1970); 100-K, 7:52:00 (1974); 100 miles, 13:33:06 (1969); 24 hours, 134.7 miles (1973).

## ❏ TRAINING PLAN

For ultramarathons, the basic run was 20 miles (2:06 to 2:36), with 30 or more miles on weekends. Shorter runs as second or third workouts in a day. One week each year, I ran 30 miles (4:15 to 4:45) daily for seven days.

## ❏ SAMPLE WEEK

Of 214 miles.

Sunday—31 miles around Manhattan Island, steady run with two speed sections.

Monday—20 miles to work.

Tuesday—A.M., 20 miles. Noon, 2.5 miles hard. P.M., 11.6 miles, hard last 3.8.

Wednesday—A.M., 20 miles. P.M., 20 miles, much slower than morning.

Thursday—A.M., 20 miles. Noon, 2.5 miles hard. P.M., 11.6 miles.

Friday—A.M., 20 miles. Noon, five miles.

Saturday—30 miles steady.

## ❏ FAVORITE WORKOUTS

For ultramarathons, my favorite was a 30-mile run. For shorter races, running up and down a hill (preferably grass)—sometimes going uphill and downhill hard, but more frequently going up easy and down hard.

# GRANDPA TED

One of my very best moments at the 1994 New York City Marathon came at the starting line. There I met Ted Corbitt, lining up almost unnoticed at the back where he could see all that he'd helped create.

If Fred Lebow is the father of the New York City Marathon, then Ted Corbitt is one of its grandfathers. And this is only one among many of Corbitt's proud descendents.

New York's 25th-anniversary book credits him for helping take the race citywide. But Corbitt insists that his suggestion was misunderstood.

"By 1975," writes Peter Gambaccini, "Ted Corbitt had decided it was time to give this marathon a fresh boost. He envisioned a competition of some sort between runners who each would represent one of New York's five boroughs. . . and mentioned his notion to his friend and fellow runner George Spitz. Legend now has it that Spitz mistakenly thought Corbitt was talking about a race that would actually be run THROUGH the five boroughs."

Pioneers seldom receive much of the later glory, but that's okay with soft-voiced Corbitt. He never sought attention for himself.

He never acted as a standard-bearer for American black long distance runners, of whom there still are few. He never directed a big race, never wrote a book (though one came out ABOUT him), never gave a major speech.

Corbitt let his contributions speak for him. They reach far beyond his own running, in which he was a 1952 Olympic marathoner and U.S. record holder at several ultradistances.

Ed Lacey

**Ted Corbitt**

In 1958, Ted was one of 10 founders of the Road Runners Club of America that would give the sport a framework when it exploded more than a decade later. He served as the first president of the New York Road Runners, which would grow into the world's biggest club, and edited the publication that would become *New York Running News*. He set up this country's first course certification program and watched it become the world's best.

John Chodes asked me to introduce his book, *Corbitt* (published in 1974 by Tafnews Press). "Among us runners," I wrote then, "Ted Corbitt is admired and envied not because he has run so well, but because he has run so well for so long. Corbitt is amazing to us because he has lasted."

He was 54 then and had run for almost 40 of those years. Little did we know that Ted's running was ending that same year. A severe case of asthma stopped him abruptly.

Corbitt had said, "Fitness can't be stored. It must be earned over and over, indefinitely." So he became a long-distance walker.

Now he says, "Sometimes I think I developed the asthma so that I would stop. I was burned out. But I had to taper off, start walking the distance because it had been like an addiction. I was afraid of quitting cold-turkey."

At almost 75 (he'll reach that birthday on January 31st, 1995), he remains quite active. Robert Lipsyte, writing in the *New York Times,* calls Ted "the last surviving spiritual elder of the modern running clan."

Lipsyte adds, "He never allowed himself to become a guru. He never had the showman's flare of Fred Lebow or Dr. George Sheehan or Jim Fixx.

"He never made money from the boom or became celebrated outside the runner's world. He just ran and ran and ran."

Corbitt now walks and walks and walks. In the New York City Marathon, yes, but also in the annual 100-mile race named for him.

Ted has revised downward his goal of living 100 years. Now he wants to celebrate the new century, which will arrive as he turns 80.

His way of getting there is as it has always been: "Keep moving. Do something useful." Few lifetimes have been filled with more movement or more useful work.

# MARK COVERT

July 22nd, 1968, Covert took a rest day. He ran the next day—and as of this writing hasn't rested again since then. During that period, he has run through a broken foot bone, on the storm-tossed deck of a cruise ship, and the day after hemorrhoid surgery. "The Streak," as he calls it, now covers about 10,000 days and 100,000-plus miles. It obscures two other features of Covert: his talents as a runner (7th in the 1972 Olympic Marathon Trial) and as a coach (at Antelope Valley College in California).

## ❏ MARK COVERT

Lancaster, California. Born November 17th, 1950, in Aurora, Illinois. 5'8", 150 pounds. Married, four children. Occupation: teacher and coach. Began racing in 1965. Self-coached.

## ❏ BEST TIMES

Mile, 4:11 (1971); two miles, 8:55 (1973); three miles, 13:41 (1972); six miles, 28:08 (1971), 15-K, 46:44 (1975); 10 miles, 48:08 (1971); one hour, 11 miles 1635 yards; 20-K, 1:02:14 (1974); half-marathon, 1:04:28; 25-K, 1:19:53 (1972); marathon, 2:22:35 (1972).

## ❏ TRAINING PLAN

I block the year into track and racing periods—using July, August and September for a base period; October and November for a racing period; December, January and February for another base period; March and April for a transition period; May and June for racing. By keeping the program at a high volume for most of the year and bringing miles down only at the end of the two racing periods, I can race at a consistently high level for most of the year.

## ❑ SAMPLE WEEK

From 1971, totaling 109 miles.

Sunday—15 miles steady.

Monday—A.M., jog two miles; 25 minutes of fartlek on a football or soccer field, changing speeds each lap; jog two miles. P.M., 8-10 miles steady.

Tuesday—A.M., six miles steady. P.M., jog two miles; 10 x 100 strides; 8 x 800 in 2:12-2:15 (2:30 rest between); jog two miles.

Wednesday—A.M., six miles steady. P.M., 10-12 miles, first 6-8 steady to hard, last four very hard.

Thursday—A.M., six miles steady. P.M., jog two miles; 8 x 100 strides; 12 x 400 in 65-67 seconds with 100 jog between; jog two miles.

Friday—A.M., six miles steady. P.M., six miles easy.

Saturday—A.M., five miles easy. P.M., race. (If not racing, 12-15 miles in morning, 6-8 miles in afternoon.)

## ❑ FAVORITE WORKOUT

I like them all!

# NAN DOAK-DAVIS

*She has led the two distinct lives as a runner that Joan Samuelson named: "B.C." (Before Child) and "A.D." (After Diapers). In the 1980s, Davis was an Olympic alternate at 10,000 meters and a national marathon champion. A broken foot sidetracked her for awhile, "then motherhood pleasantly took me out of running for almost two more years," she says. Returning to competition as a 33-year-old in 1995, Davis was soon PRing on the track again.*

## ❏ NANETTE L. DOAK-DAVIS

Madison, Wisconsin. Born March 7th, 1962, in Ottumwa, Iowa. 4'11³/4", 94 pounds. Married to Olympic wrestler Barry Davis, one child. Occupation: wife and mom. Began racing in 1978. Runs for Adidas. Coach: Peter Tegen.

## ❏ BEST TIMES

1500, 4:15 (1989); 3000, 8:58 (1995); 5000, 15:33 (1988); 10,000, 32:14 (1988); marathon, 2:33:11 (1989).

## ❏ TRAINING PLAN

Since taking a couple of years off and gaining a new coach, the approach has changed. (I had been coached over the phone for a few years and knew I needed a coach I could meet with.) Not having enough time to build a good base, I felt I needed to get my speed back first. This is why I quickly returned to the track. If time and body allow, I'll build a base for the marathon.

## ❏ SAMPLE WEEK

Of 53 miles, from May 1995.

Sunday—10 miles with friend Jean Oldenburg.

Monday—A.M., three miles. P.M., (indoors because weather was bad, on track larger than 200 meters); two-mile warmup; strides; 2 x 3 laps; five-minute rest; 16 x diagonals of track; two-mile warmdown.

Tuesday—48 minutes with 6 x 30-second pickups.

Wednesday—A.M., three miles. P.M., 2.5-mile warmup; strides; 2 x 300; five-minute rest; 8 x 200 in 33 seconds; five-minute rest; 5 x 300 in 50 seconds; 2.5-mile warmdown.

Thursday—A.M., three miles. Injured wrist gardening and took afternoon off.

Friday—seven miles, with Barry and Amanda riding the bike next to me; we stopped to throw rocks into the lake. Traveled to Peoria, Illinois, with Amanda.

Saturday—5-K race in Peoria, used as a tempo run.

❏ FAVORITE WORKOUT

The Sunday group run with Jean Oldenburg, Dennis Bronte and Eileen Thompson. We are all 30-something, with varied interests, and running is a serious hobby for all of us.

# MISTI DEMKO

■ *You might ask, "Why are so few runners under 30 included in this book?" The quick answer: They have better things to do in their 20s than run the roads. Demko, for instance, competed at shorter distances for 12 years before entering her first road race. Then while alternating between track and roads, she made the 1995 Pan-American Games team in the track 5000—and broke 33 minutes in a road 10-K.*

## ❑ MISTI DEMKO

Hershey, Pennsylvania. Born October 18th, 1967, in Valparaiso, Indiana. 5'4", 108 pounds. Married, no children. Occupation: graduate student. Began racing in 1979. Runs for Asics. Coach: Mike Demko.

## ❑ BEST TIMES

1500, 4:22 (1994); track 5000, 16:04 (1995); road 5-K, 15:50 (1993); 10-K, 32:43 (1994); 12-K, 40:45 (1994); 15-K, 51:41 (1994).

## ❑ TRAINING PLAN

Because of my history of back injuries (since 1990) and compartment syndrome (requiring surgery in 1995), it has been necessary for me to get the most quality I can out of the lowest optimal mileage. Typically, I train 50 to 55 miles per week with two quality sessions, three days at 6:20 to 6:30 pace and two slow, easy days.

## ❑ SAMPLE WEEK

Of 55 miles, prior to my 10-K PR in 1994.

Sunday—7.5 miles, moderate pace (6:30).

Monday—10 miles easy (6:45) with striders.

Tuesday—A.M., three miles. P.M., six miles moderate (6:30).

Wednesday—two-mile warmup; 4 x 800 in 2:30, jog 2:00 between; 4 x 400 in 73 seconds, jog 1:00 between; two-mile warmdown.

Thursday—A.M., three miles. P.M., seven miles easy (6:40-6:45).

Friday—four miles moderate.

Saturday—two-mile warmup; 1500 in 4:33; five-minute recovery; 10-minute steady state run on road; 1.5-mile warmdown.

## ❏ FAVORITE WORKOUT

One I read about in *Running Research News:* 400 fast, 400 slow, 300 fast, 300 slow, 200 fast, 200 slow, 100 fast, 100 slow—then repeat to equal 5000 in 17:00. This teaches me to run fast TIRED.

# PATTI DILLON

*Don't recognize the name? Try "Catalano" in place of Dillon. For a period centered on 1980, Patti almost had the road sport to herself in the U.S. while setting national records at eight distances. She was the first American marathoner to break 2:30. See details on her more recent life in the sidebar.*

❏ **PATTI DILLON (formerly Catalano)**

Hyde Park, Massachusetts. Born April 6th, 1953, in Chelsea, Massachusetts. 5'4½", 104 pounds. Married, one child. Occupation: homemaker. Began racing in 1976. Ran for Athletics West and Boston AA. Coaches: Joe Catalano, Bill Squires, self.

❏ **BEST TIMES**

Mile, 4:51; five miles, 25:48; 10-K, 32:04; 15-K, 49:33; 10 miles, 53:40; 20-K, 1:08:40; half-marathon, 1:14:10; 30-K, 1:44:42; marathon, 2:27:51.

❏ **TRAINING PLAN**

I had one intense training year, 1980-81, the only year I trained through the winter. The early years, 1976-79, I took off two to three months--tired, didn't like winter running, also injured sometimes. I liked to do two or three intense workouts a week—hills, fartlek, track, something quicker. Otherwise, I would always run slow like now.

❏ **SAMPLE WEEK**

Of 104 to 110 miles.

Sunday—A.M., long run. P.M., short run.

**Patti (Catalano) Dillon at her peak in the 70's.**

Monday—A.M., one hour easy. P.M., one hour easy.

Tuesday—A.M., one hour easy. P.M., hills, track or fartlek.

Wednesday—A.M., 1:20-1:30 easy. P.M., one hour easy.

Thursday—A.M., one hour easy. P.M., hills, track or fartlek.

Friday—A.M., one hour easy. P.M., one hour easy.

Saturday—one hour easy and/or race.

❑ **FAVORITE WORKOUTS**

(1) Long, long run with "the guys" when I'm fit—three hours or more. (2) Repeat miles on fall evenings.

# THE NEW PATTI

I first saw the new Patti Catalano two summers ago at the Asbury Park 10-K. We happened to sit together during the awards program at an open-air bandshell overlooking the Jersey Shore.

She's never looked better. Gone was the gauntness of the early 1980s when she was America's top road racer.

Patti looked in the best of health. That, of course, isn't the same as being racing fit.

She was called to the stage to collect a prize in her age group. The announced time, a minute per mile slower than her best, reminded Patti of the runner she had been a few years earlier.

"I'm so embe-e-erressed!" she said to her friends, drawing out the last word and giving it her richest Boston accent.

She had no reason to be embarrassed. She was a bigger winner now than she had ever been in her glory years.

I didn't yet know about the fight she was waging, and winning. This spring, she chose to make her problem public. She admitted it in two articles by Katherine Williams.

Patti had slipped into bulimia—a cycle of starving, overeating and then throwing up—in 1978. She'd binged and purged "five or six times a day" during the period when she set her national road records.

She talks some about her recovery in a *Running Times* article. Williams supplies details in *Boston Magazine*: "She broke the cycle without professional help, depending largely on the same inner strength that had previously taken her to the top of women's running."

Patti says, "My anxieties and self-determination drove me. It was the greatest race, victory—whatever—of my life.

"I had hit bottom, and I chose to come out of it. Nothing can compare. Nothing."

A new dream is taking shape. That is, writes Katherine Williams, "opening a small group home for women recovering from bulimia. The simple things—stacking wood, caring for animals, gardening—would help rebuild self-esteem. Catalano's own road back to health began when she forced herself to do things as ordinary as getting up each day and showering."

And running. "For me, to run again is great," says Patti. "To compete again is better, and to have big ambitions is better, too.

"I want to see what I can do with a healthy body and through clean living. I'm not talking about a rigid life style where you don't even drink coffee. I'm talking about good, honest living, with lots of love and giving."

She was comfortable enough with her new self to run the 1988 Boston Marathon, and face its demanding media and crowds, the same month the confessional articles appeared. At 2:57, Patti was slower by 30 minutes than she'd run here in 1981. But in the important ways, she is doing much better now. She isn't embarrassed to be seen now.

"The best thing that can happen from all this is that someone with a bulimia problem will see or hear me," she tells writer Williams. "I want to help others recover, because they're reaching out for something the way I was. I am going to run well again, and I am going to be heard."

(Patti's recovery took a different, and better, turn than she'd planned when this story was written. She is married to Dan Dillon, a former international runner himself, and became the mother of a son.)

# NANCY DITZ

*Ditz's career was about as perfect as one gets: first American, New York City Marathon, 1983. . . first American, World Cup Marathon, 1985. . . first American, World Championships Marathon, 1987. . . first American, Olympic Marathon, 1988. . . 12 years of racing, no injuries. Now retired as a competitor, she contributes as a TV reporter and USATF official.*

## ❏ NANCY DITZ

Woodside, California. Born June 25th, 1954, in San Jose, California. 5'6", 114 pounds. Married, two children. Occupation: self-employed. Began racing in 1980, retired 1992.

## ❏ BEST TIMES

10-K, 32:45; half-marathon, 1:12:46; marathon, 2:30:14.

## ❏ TRAINING PLAN

Key elements: consistency and relatively high mileage (up to 120 miles per week). My times at all distances kept dropping as my average weekly mileage increased. If I were training now, the mileage would be higher because I now believe I could have handled more volume.

## ❏ SAMPLE WEEK

From April 1988, about one month before setting a PR in Olympic Marathon Trial and qualifying for the Seoul Games.

Monday—A.M., five miles. P.M., 10 miles.

Tuesday—A.M., five miles. P.M., 6 x 1000, 1 x 400.

Wednesday—A.M., five miles. P.M., nine miles, hill circuit.

**Nancy Ditz**

Thursday—A.M., five miles. P.M., 3000 time trial.

Friday—nine miles, hill circuit.

Saturday—A.M., five miles. P.M., three miles on track, alternating laps of 85 and 74-75 seconds.

Sunday—two-hour 10-minute run.

## ❏ FAVORITE WORKOUT

6-8 x 1000 at sub-3:05 with 600 jog between. Long enough and fast enough to keep me interested. This workout is FUN!

# JEROME DRAYTON

*If he'd lived a little farther south—say, just below the Canadian border—he would be lionized now as men named Shorter and Rodgers are. The U.S. seems to do better at legend-making than Canada, where Drayton now gets little attention. This despite holding his national marathon record continuously for more than a quarter-century, setting the current mark of 2:10:09 in 1975, ranking first in the world in '69, winning Boston in '77, running in two Olympics, and once holding the world record for 10 miles on the track.*

## ❏ JEROME PETER DRAYTON

Toronto, Ontario. Born January 10th, 1945, in Kolbermoor, Germany. 5'9", 132 pounds. Single. Occupation: civil servant. Began racing in 1963. Ran for Toronto Olympic Club. Coach: Paul Poce and self.

## ❏ BEST TIMES

3000, 7:57.0 (1975); two miles, 8:45.6 (1970); three miles, 13:06.0 (1975); 5000, 13:34.9 (1975); 10,000, 28:13.8 (1975); 10 miles, 46:37.6 (1970); marathon, 2:10:09 (1975).

## ❏ TRAINING PLAN

(Rather than comment specificially on his own training, Drayton sent a lengthy and well-considered collection of advice for other runners. Excerpts follow.)

The best way to start training is to understand the vital processes of the body—at least those that relate directly to running. If you understand some of your body's inner workings, and are sensitive to its needs and states of tiredness, it can perform magnificently for you. Without such sensitivity, you can too easily push yourself into pain, injury or fatigue. With a little fine-tuning, however, most of us can make training safer and more productive.

The best training program for you is one that meets your particular needs. This applies to beginners as well as to world-class runners. Don't adopt the successful program of friends. Although they may be succeeding, they may be improving IN SPITE OF their program. It's fine to try new training ideas, but experiment with only one at a time. Then blend the successful ones into your program to fit your own demands, rest needs and current level of performance.

Some training principles:

- **RECOVERY,** the most important principle. Hard or long runs must always be followed by easy days (usually two to three) in which the pace or distance is reduced.

- **OVERLOAD.** Workload must be sufficiently demanding to encourage the body to adapt and improve performance capacity.

- **PROGRESSION.** Workload must gradually increase as the runner's body adapts to previous loadings.

- **SPECIFICITY.** Training load must relate to the runner's present level of fitness and his or her competitive event.

- **REVERSIBILITY.** The rate at which performance capacity is lost will be similar to the rate at which it was gained.

The annual training program is divided into four distinct periods:

1. **TRANSITION.** A period of recuperation, during which the runner recovers from the fatigue of the previous competition period.

2. **GENERAL PREPARATION.** Foundation training during which aerobic fitness, mobility, strength and local muscular endurance are developed. These allow the runner to accept and benefit from specific forms of training.

3. **SPECIAL PREPARATION.** Training to develop the spe-

cific fitness required to meet the demands of the runner's event.

4.  **COMPETITION.** Training aimed at preparing the runner for an important race or series of races.

# JANICE ETTLE

For all the inequities that once existed between the sexes in running, women now have an option that men don't. It's possible for a woman to have qualified for all four of the Olympic Marathon Trials, 1984 to '96. Ettle is one of the few runners with a perfect record. Twice she has placed in the top 10 at the Trials, in a career that has also taken her to the World Cup and Pan-American Games.

## ❏ JANICE ETTLE

St. Paul, Minnesota. Born December 3rd, 1958, in Freeport, Minnesota. 5'7", 128 pounds. Single. Occupation: medical laboratory technician. Began racing in 1973. Self-coached.

## ❏ BEST TIMES

Mile, 4:48 (1988); 3000, 9:31 (1992); track 5000, 16:21 (1992); road 5-K, 16:00 (1992); 8-K, 26:23 (1988); track 10,000, 33:25 (1992); road 10-K, 33:13 (1988); 15-K, 51:20 (1988); 20-K, 1:10:08 (1990); half-marathon, 1:12:01 (1984); 25-K, 1:29:11 (1985); marathon, 2:33:41 (1984).

## ❏ TRAINING PLAN

Four phases: (1) base-mileage training; (2) hill-strength training; (3) endurance speed; (4) sharpening. Each phase is approximately four weeks. I do base and hills during the Minnesota winter; phases three and four in spring, and again in fall.

## ❏ SAMPLE WEEK

Due to my work schedule, I don't follow a seven-day schedule. Mileage varies from 60 to 100 a week, plus weights, swimming and cycling.

Sunday—long run of 20-25 miles; or 15-mile fartlek or hills.

Monday—easy eight miles.

Tuesday—12-16-mile fartlek or hills; or 8-10-mile track workout.

Wednesday—easy 5-10 miles.

Thursday—long run if not taken on Sunday; or 10-15-mile fartlek; or track workout.

Friday—easy.

Saturday—race; or 8-10 miles aerobic fartlek or hills.

## ❏ FAVORITE WORKOUT

Each has its purpose in a planned schedule. I like my 15-milers with 3-4 x 20 minutes moderately hard, two minutes easy. This is excellent for marathon preparation.

# GARY FANELLI

> It would be too easy to typecast Fanelli as a "stunt runner." Easy and wrong. Oh, he certainly gained a measure of fame for racing in costume. More quietly and seriously, though, he ran impressively without disguises. He set the pace for the first half of the 1980 Olympic Marathon Trial, the same year he ran 2:14. Later, he moved to American Samoa to qualify for the Seoul Games.

## ❏ GARY M. FANELLI

Ardsley, Pennsylvania. Born October 24th, 1950, in Philadelphia. 6'2", 158 pounds. Married, two children. Occupation: artist. Began racing in 1960. Runs for Reebok and Anorexic Sumo Track Club. Self-coached.

## ❏ BEST TIMES

Mile, 4:10 (1977); 3000, 8:15 (1977); 5000, 14:06 (1979); 10,000, 29:04 (1981); half-marathon, 1:02:54 (1981); marathon, 2:14:16 (1980).

## ❏ TRAINING PLAN

I go in harmony with the four seasons. Even while living in Hawaii, I kept the same seasonal rhythms: winter—resting, recovering and rebuilding; spring—higher mileage and more tempo as racing time nears; summer—I'm in full swing, racing and training fast; fall—still racing but less often, feeling weary as the season winds down.

## ❏ SAMPLE WEEK

This entry comes after months and years of steady buildup preparation, with most weeks over 100 miles and some upwards of 150, and lots of racing. The actual log entry from a week in August-September 1980 totals 104 miles with several tapering days, leading to marathon PR of 2:14:16 in Montreal on the day after this week ended.

Sunday—A.M., four miles easy. P.M., 20 miles in 2:12, good effort.

Monday—A.M., four miles easy. P.M., 11 miles, good effort.

Tuesday—A.M., half-marathon race in 1:08:11, very hot. P.M., four miles.

Wednesday—six miles easy.

Thursday—five miles easy.

Friday—A.M., four miles. P.M., five miles.

Saturday—four miles easy.

## ❏ FAVORITE WORKOUT

Ten-mile hill run on Mount Tantalus in Hawaii. I enjoyed the five miles up to the top and could run a long, hard, sustained pace or interval surges on the really hilly parts. This workout helped my racing tremendously and was most scenic on the way down.

# BARBARA FILUTZE

*Runners typically enter their masters years at their best. Performances then fall off gradually, and the runner soon falls out of contention as new masters come in at THEIR best. Filutze wasn't typical. Though she started racing at 33 and competed in the first Olympic Marathon Trial at 37, she set many PRs—dozens of them age-group and single-age U.S. records—in her 40s and kept winning races throughout that decade.*

## ❏ BARBARA FILUTZE

Erie, Pennsylvania. Born June 21st, 1946, in Erie. 5'1½", 100 pounds. Married, three children, one grandchild. Occupation: runner, trainer, high school cross country and track coach. Began racing in 1979. Runs for Reebok. Coach: husband Mike and self.

## ❏ BEST TIMES

3000, 10:19.9 (1989); 5-K, 16:58 (1987); 8-K, 28:03 (1993); 10-K, 33:36 (1986); 15-K, 54:12 (1987); half-marathon, 1:16:00 (1989); marathon, 2:41:18 (1984).

## ❏ TRAINING PLAN

I try to train to the best of my ability at the time. Things change, and I have to adjust to every passing year. I'm always looking for new techniques and training help to get every advantage. My goal is to compete in masters as long as possible.

## ❏ SAMPLE WEEK

Of 70-plus miles.

Sunday—10-K race, 16 miles for day; or long run of 16-18 miles.

Monday—A.M., four miles with 6 x 20-second striders. P.M., four miles.

Tuesday—A.M., eight miles on hills with 6 x 20-second sprints. P.M., two miles.

Wednesday—10 miles, including 5 x mile.

Thursday—eight miles with 6 x 20-second striders.

Friday—13 miles, including 6 x half-mile.

Saturday—10 miles on hills with 10 x 20-second sprints.

❑ FAVORITE WORKOUTS.

For speed: five repeat miles on a road with a slight hill; three repeats downhill, two uphill. For strength or hill race: three sets of $3^1/_2$ minutes downhill, $5^1/_2$ minutes uphill loop, sprint 100 meters at top.

# TOM FLEMING

■ *A gratifying number of top runners from the 1970s continue to contribute in other ways. Some write, some broadcast, some tour as goodwill ambassadors. And many give the most direct type of help—as coaches. Fleming won two New York City Marathons and finished second twice at Boston in the '70s. Later, he started a running store that became a coaching base. His most prominent coachee is Anne Marie Lauck (featured later in this book).*

❏ **TOM FLEMING**

Bloomfield, New Jersey. Born July 23rd, 1951, in Long Branch, New Jersey. 6'1", 155 pounds. Married, two children. Occupation: coaching and sales. Began racing in 1968. Runs for Adidas Running Room. Self-coached.

❏ **BEST TIMES**

5000, 14:07; 10,000, 28:48; half-marathon, 1:04:12; 30-K, 1:30:27; 20 miles, 1:40:21; marathon, 2:12:05.

❏ **TRAINING PLAN**

Build a huge distance base over several years. Don't push the speed workouts. Use tempo runs and fartlek workouts on hard days, instead of many hard reps on the track all the time.

❏ **SAMPLE WEEK**

Of "God knows how many miles" during prime racing years.

Sunday—A.M., longish run, 20-21 miles at 6:00-6:10 pace. P.M., easy run, 10 miles at 6:20 pace.

Monday—A.M., easy run, eight miles. P.M., steady effort, 8-10 miles.

Tuesday—A.M., six-mile run. P.M., two-mile warmup; 6 x mile, 4:35-4:40, with 400 between.

Wednesday—A.M., 10 miles steady. P.M., 10 miles steady.

Thursday—A.M., six-mile run, easy. P.M., 15-mile run, good effort.

Friday—A.M., 10-mile run, relaxed. P.M., 10-mile run, moderate effort.

Saturday—A.M., 10 miles with four miles in 19:00 enroute. P.M., easy 6-8 miles.

## ❏ FAVORITE WORKOUTS

A.M., 10-mile run at 6:00 pace. P.M., 6 x mile in 4:40. Basic 20-mile day!

# JACK FOSTER

It's a telling oversight that Foster's questionnaire doesn't mention the mark for which we now know him best: the 2:11:19 marathon at age 41. That time stood for 16 years as a world masters record—though he didn't acknowledge that fact, either. Foster did say what meant more to him: placing second in Commonwealth Games Marathon, competing in two Olympics, running in three World Cross Country Championships and setting a world OPEN best for 20 miles on the track—all after his 39th birthday.

❏ **JACK FOSTER**

Rotorua, New Zealand. Born May 23rd, 1932, in Liverpool, England. 5'9", 138 pounds. Married, four children. Occupation: administration, public works. Began racing in 1965. Self-coached.

❏ **BEST TIMES**

Track 5000, 13:55 (1973); track 10,000, 28:46 (1972); 10 miles, 47:42 (1976); 20 miles, 1:39:15 (1971); marathon, 2:11:19 (1974).

❏ **TRAINING PLAN**

Pretty casual. Ran after work each day, mostly cross-country farmlands and forest trails, very hilly. Ran on a horse-race track one day most weeks, anything from three to 10 one-mile reps, pretty quick, 4:50-ish with half-mile jog recovery. This and long Sunday run of 1½ to 2¼ hours would be the key elements, I guess.

❏ **SAMPLE WEEK**

Of about 70 miles.

**Jack Foster**

Sunday—1¹/₂ to 2¹/₄ hours on farmlands, forest trails and/or roads.

Monday—easy 30-45 minutes on grass parkland.

Tuesday—60-75 minutes on farmlands, or one-mile reps on horse-race track.

Wednesday—easy 30-45 minutes on grass parkland.

Thursday—60-75 minutes on farmlands.

Friday—rest.

Saturday—usually a club race: two- to five-mile road run, seven-mile cross country or road relay.

## ❑ FAVORITE WORKOUT

Mile reps on horse-race track, because it was something different.

# NORM FRANK

When Sy Mah died in 1988, he had run 524 marathons. This was a record thought at the time to be unbeatable. But within six years, Norm Frank had beaten it. Frank planned to run his 600th at the 1996 Boston, and his total could top 1000 before he runs his last marathon. He said when contacted about appearing in this book, "I'm not sure you would want to use me. I'm not much on training." His weekly marathons ARE his training.

❏ **NORMAN FRANK**

Rochester, New York. Born June 20th, 1931, in Rochester. 6'2", 180 pounds. Single, two children. Occupation: landscaper. Began racing in 1967. Runs for Rochester Track Club. Self-coached.

❏ **BEST TIMES**

5-K, 21:20 (1971); 10-K, 40:10 (1969); marathon, 3:20 (1970); 50 miles, 7:56 (1972).

❏ **TRAINING PLAN**

Because I run three or four marathons a month, I do very little training. I believe this is why I have run injury-free for 29 years.

❏ **SAMPLE WEEK**

Of 31 to 37 miles.

Sunday—marathon (or rest if I ran one on Saturday).

Monday—rest.

Tuesday—upper-body weight training; maybe three miles

easy.

Wednesday—five miles easy.

Thursday—upper-body weight training; maybe three miles easy.

Friday—rest.

Saturday—marathon (or rest if running one on Sunday).

❏ **FAVORITE WORKOUT**

Wednesday five-mile. It works out any soreness.

# JEFF GALLOWAY

So much has Galloway done in and around this sport, and for so long, that we need a separate story to cover it all. See his sidebar.

❏ **JEFF GALLOWAY**

Atlanta, Georgia. Born July 12th, 1945, in Raleigh, North Carolina. 5'11", 138 pounds. Married, two children. Occupation: teacher-coach. Began racing in 1958.

❏ **BEST TIMES**

Two miles, 8:32 (1972); 5000, 13:41 (1972); 10,000, 28:29 (1972 and '73); marathon, 2:16 (1980).

❏ **TRAINING PLAN (current)**

Go out slowly. Regular form accelerations, twice a week. Long runs every other week, every third week for marathon. Keep it fun!

❏ **SAMPLE WEEK**

Of 50 miles.

Sunday—A.M., one mile easy; 800 meters of accelerations; 5-K race; two-mile warmdown. P.M., five miles slow.

Monday—A.M., seven miles easy. P.M., five miles easy.

Tuesday—no running; swimming and strength exercises.

Wednesday—A.M., seven miles easy. P.M., five miles with 8-12 accelerations (100-300 meters).

Thursday—A.M., seven miles easy. P.M., five miles with hill repeats and accelerations.

**Jeff Galloway**

Friday—no running; swimming and strength exercises.

Saturday—long and easy, 15-20 miles.

## ❏ FAVORITE WORKOUT

Seven to eight miles of fartlek. I mold it to prepare for the current race.

# JEFF OF ALL TRADES

We joined a dinner-in-progress at a Winnipeg pasta restaurant the night before the Manitoba Marathon. We checked in with the hostess by saying, "We're with a running group but don't know whose name it's under."

"Galloway," she said. "The others are already seated. Come this way."

The only Galloway I knew was Jeff. I knew he was 2000 miles away in Atlanta.

But these were his students, and they honored him this night by adopting his name. They would graduate the next morning from his marathon training program.

The Winnipeg group is one of 17 to sprout across the continent. All follow the Galloway program and receive at least one visit from Jeff himself. Come to think of it, he might now reach more runners, more places and in more ways than anyone else in the sport.

Jeff Galloway was one of the lesser-known members in the Olympic class of 1972. He wasn't a gold medalist like Frank Shorter, or a near-medalist like Kenny Moore and Steve Prefontaine, a child star like Francie Larrieu or a world champion like Doris Brown, a fallen hero like Jim Ryun or a Boston winner-to-be like Jon Anderson.

Many of these Olympians still play one or two roles brilliantly in the sport. Shorter and Ryun are famous for being themselves, Moore has become the sport's standard-setting writer, Larrieu has gone from youngest to oldest Olympian, and Jack Bacheler, Francie Kraker Goodridge, Doug Brown, Doris Brown Heritage and Mike Manley all have coached at high levels.

But no one from this illustrious class has shown more versatility and staying power than Galloway. In fact, no one in this sport plays as many roles so well.

Galloway the Teacher, who touches runners in person with his marathon program and at other race clinics, is only one of those roles. He is also Galloway the Runner, the Store Owner, the Race Promoter, the Camp Director, the Communicator.

Runner Galloway won the first Peachtree Road Race, which celebrated its 25th running this summer. Jeff, who can still squeeze a 33-minute 10-K from his 30-mile training weeks, hoped to be competitive in his age group (he's 49) at the anniversary race.

"Then I hurt a calf muscle, my first injury in nine years," he says. Jeff still ran with his 12-year-old son Brennan.

Store Owner Galloway operates the original Phidippides running shop in Atlanta. It once anchored a nationwide string of franchises with the same name but now is a single shop, one of the oldest and best in the business.

Race Promoter Galloway directs events through his other company, Galloway Productions. Many of the races are corporate, including a 14,000-runner event in Atlanta that's part of a national series sponsored by Office Depot.

Camp Director Galloway has organized running "vacations" (as he likes to call them) at Lake Tahoe since the 1970s. These have spread as far as New England and the Bahamas.

Communicator Galloway works equally well over the air and on paper, while reporting events or giving advice. He delivers race commentary on television and radio, and one publication isn't big enough to hold all of his writing.

Jeff appears regularly in *Running Times, RRCA Footnotes* and many regional magazines. His one book has shown remarkable endurance in an arena where most books are sprinters that burn out quickly.

*Galloway's Book of Running* has lasted a dozen years. He has sold more copies than any author on this subject who isn't named Fixx or Sheehan.

Readers and publishers would like to see another volume. Jeff surely has enough experiences to write from.

(Galloway celebrated his 50th birthday in 1995 by releasing his second book, *Return of the Tribes.*)

# JACQUELINE GAREAU

*Meet the REAL winner of the 1980 Boston Marathon. Full glory for that moment was stolen from Gareau by someone whose name we still can't mention without gagging. Gareau was authentic—a Canadian trailblazer on par with Patti Catalano or Joan Benoit in the States. Gareau was her country's first sub-2:30 woman marathoner—and first female winner at Boston.*

## ❏ JACQUELINE GAREAU

St. Bruno, Quebec. Born March 10th, 1953, in L'Annonciation, Quebec. 5'2", 98 pounds. Married, one child. Occupation: runner, now mother. Began racing in 1977. Runs for Reebok. Coach: Gilles LaPierre.

## ❏ BEST TIMES

Track 5000, 16:04 (1985); road 5-K, 16:10 (1986); 10-K, 33:05 (1985); 15-K, 49:56 (1985); marathon, 2:29:27 (1983).

## ❏ TRAINING PLAN

Goal: marathon. Objectives: (1) aerobic endurance with long runs, medium-pace runs, marathon-pace runs; (2) aerobic power with fast runs (continuous and interval), road races.

## ❏ SAMPLE WEEK

From March 1983, one month before marathon PR of 2:29:27 at Boston; week's total about 115 miles.

Sunday—A.M., two hours 30 minutes on hilly course with 3 x 12 minutes on hills at marathon pace; finished strong. P.M., 30 minutes easy on grass.

**Jacqueline Gareau**

Monday—A.M., 40 minutes on grass; felt quite good. P.M., 45 minutes of weights.

Tuesday—A.M., 35 minutes easy. P.M., 25-minute warmup; 8 x 800 in 2:33-2:35 with 400 jog between; 22-minute warmdown.

Wednesday—A.M., 40 minutes; felt good, no stiffness. P.M., 40 minutes, good pace (6:30 per mile).

Thursday—A.M., one hour 45 minutes hilly fartlek with 6 x five minutes at 10-K pace, three-minute recovery. P.M., 30 minutes easy.

Friday—60 minutes hilly; weights.

Saturday—two hours five minutes with 3 x 12 minutes at marathon pace on hills; last mile on track in 6:00; felt strong.

## ❏ FAVORITE WORKOUT

Long run with 3 x 12 minutes at marathon pace. Combination of long run and marathon pace gives me a lot of endurance and strength.

# TIM GARGIULO

*Just wait. That's hard advice for a young runner to follow when he might want everything now. Gargiulo was gifted enough in his mid-20s to tap the lucrative world of 10-K and beyond. But he limited his road racing in distance and number, while tapping other options as one of the leading young Americans in cross country (top U.S. finisher at the 1994 Worlds) and track. Just wait; he'll mature on the roads. He has plenty of time for that.*

## ❏ TIMOTHY JOHN GARGIULO

Dallas, Texas. Born February 2nd, 1968, in Milwaukee, Wisconsin. 5'10", 135 pounds. Married. Occupation: attorney. Began racing in 1987. Runs for Brooks Republic of Texas Racing Team. Coach: Terry Jessup.

## ❏ BEST TIMES

1500, 3:43 (1992); road mile, 3:55 (1992); track 5000, 13:42 (1995); road 5-K, 13:27 (1992); four miles, 17:53 (1995).

## ❏ TRAINING PLAN

Base training in fall to get ready for cross country. In February, major hill training. To the track, March through July. Then a few weeks' rest.

## ❏ SAMPLE WEEK

Of 75-85 miles.

Sunday—long easy run, 14-18 miles depending on time of year.

Monday—A.M., 10 miles easy and weights. P.M., five miles easy.

Tuesday—two-mile warmup; four sets of 2 x 800 with one-minute rest between intervals, four minutes between sets; two-mile cooldown.

Wednesday—A.M., 10 miles easy and weights. P.M., five miles easy.

Thursday—two-mile warmup; 10 x 600 with 75 seconds rest between; two-mile cooldown.

Friday—five miles easy and weights.

Saturday—race or hill session with intervals (e.g., 5 x one minute hard, one easy; 8 x 30 seconds hard, 30 easy), totaling about 75 minutes with warmup and cooldown; totaling about 75 minutes).

## ❏ FAVORITE WORKOUT

The hill sessions (during Febuary) are probably the most valuable because of the combination of strength and speed they build. But they are also the most difficult.

# MIKI GORMAN

Her story became a movie: born in China of Japanese parents, a wartime childhood, emigre' to the U.S. as a young adult, then the running. . . Gorman's first races were ultras on an indoor track at her health club. She didn't enter an open road race until her 38th year, but soon afterward set a world marathon record of 2:46:36. Gorman won Boston and New York City (twice) after turning 40.

## ❏ MICHIKO SUWA GORMAN

Los Angeles, California. Born August 9th, 1935, in Chigtau, China. 5'1", 90 pounds. Divorced, one child. Occupation: secretary. Began racing in 1969. Ran for Los Angeles Athletic Club and San Fernando Valley Track Club. Coaches: Luan Dosti and Laszlo Tabori.

## ❏ BEST TIMES

1500, 4:39 (1977); 5000, 16:57 (1977); five miles, 28:02 (1978); 10-K, 35:26 (1978); half-marathon, 1:15:58 (1978); marathon, 2:39:11 (1976); 100 miles, 21:04 (1969).

## ❏ TRAINING PLAN

About 60 mile-per-week average throughout the year, combined with speedwork. Gradually increase mileage up to 100-120 before major marathons, twice a year.

## ❏ SAMPLE WEEK

Of 70 to 100 miles.

Sunday—20 miles or more.

Monday—A.M., 10-K easy. P.M., 8-10-mile tempo run.

Tuesday—A.M., 10-K easy. P.M. speedwork on track (typical workout would be 6 x 200, 4 x 400, 10 x 150)

Wednesday—A.M., 10-K easy. P.M., 8-10 miles easy.

Thursday—A.M., 10-K easy. P.M., speedwork on track (same as Tuesday).

Friday—A.M., 10-K easy. P.M., 10 miles plus either fartlek hillwork or tempo run.

Saturday—A.M., 10-K easy. P.M., 10 miles plus either tempo run or fartlek hillwork.

## ❏ FAVORITE WORKOUT

Fartlek on a cross country course, because it makes me feel free and it's fun.

Miki Gorman

# NORM GREEN

*Like many runners of his vintage, Green has enjoyed two widely spaced running careers. He ran early, "retired" young, then returned almost three decades later. Green's competitive revival came at age 49. He ran a 32:09 10-K and a 2:25:51 marathon in his 50s.*

## ❏ NORMAN M. GREEN JR.

Wayne, Pennsylvania. Born June 27th, 1932, in Oakland, California. 5'10", 145 pounds. Married, four children. Occupation: clergy. Began racing in 1952, returned after long hiatus in 1981. Self-coached.

## ❏ BEST TIMES

Mile, 4:24.0 (1951); 3000, 9:16.8 (1988); 5-K, 16:23 (1981); five miles, 25:42 (1984); 10-K, 32:09 (1983); 15-K, 49:14 (1984); 10 miles, 52:53 (1983); 20-K, 1:05:50 (1983); 20-K, 1:05:50 (1983); half-marathon, 1:09:30 (1984); 25-K, 1:21:44 (1983); 30-K, 1:46:33 (1988); marathon, 2:25:51 (1984).

## ❏ TRAINING PLAN

Almost all mileage is tempo training, hard-easy, accomplished by varying the distance from three miles to 15 miles—with five to eight as major emphasis. Marathon preparation includes one to four 20-mile runs. In the past five years, I have generally included one rest day a week.

## ❏ SAMPLE WEEK

In August-September 1987, about a month before running 2:27:42 at Twin Cities Marathon; age 55.

Sunday—five miles at 5:53 pace.

Monday—10 miles at 5:40 pace.

Tuesday—five miles at 5:47 pace; Nautilus circuit at fitness center.

Wednesday—seven miles at 5:42 pace.

Thursday—five miles at 5:24 pace; Nautilus circuit.

Friday—five miles at 5:35 pace.

Saturday—20 miles at 5:51 pace.

## ❏ FAVORITE WORKOUT

Seven-mile loop through Valley Forge National Park. It includes rolling terrain and enough distance to maximize strength training. I pace this run at 10 to 15 seconds over 10-mile race pace.

# JIM HAGE

*If you think runners take themselves and their sport too seriously, you need to read the newsletter that Hage co-produces.* Running, Ranting & Racing *(R3 for short) delivers an irreverent, often politically incorrect take on the sport. But behind its barbs lie the unmistakable expertise born of Hage's 20-plus years of running, including a 2:15 marathon.*

❏ **JAMES D. HAGE**

Lanham, Maryland. Born February 8th, 1958, in Washington, DC. 5'10", 148 pounds. Single. Occupation: lawyer. Began racing in 1973. Runs for Washington Running Club. Coach: Charles Torpey.

❏ **BEST TIMES**

10-K, 29:22 (1992); half-marathon, 1:04:30 (1987); marathon, 2:15:52 (1992).

❏ **TRAINING PLAN**

Base: 100 to 120 miles per week. Prior to marathon: six long runs up to 23 miles; track or tempo work once or twice a week for 10 weeks.

❏ **SAMPLE WEEK**

Of 108 miles.

Sunday—20-23 miles.

Monday—A.M., five miles. P.M., nine miles.

Tuesday—A.M., five miles. P.M., 10 miles.

Wednesday—A.M., five miles. P.M., four-mile warmup; 4 x

mile in 4:40-4:46; three-mile cooldown.

Thursday—A.M., five miles. P.M., eight miles.

Friday—A.M., five miles. P.M., eight miles.

Saturday—A.M., 10 miles including 5-K tempo run. P.M., six miles.

## ❏ FAVORITE WORKOUT

Four-mile warmup; one mile in 4:36; jog quarter; four-mile tempo run; jog quarter; one mile fast; cooldown. This stimulates surging in a race and running fast while tired.

# JACQUELINE HANSEN

When Joan Benoit won the first Olympic Marathon for women, she paid tribute to the foremothers of the sport. She mentioned Jacqueline Hansen by name. And no wonder. In the 10 years prior to the Los Angeles Games, Hansen became the first woman to break 2:45 (in 1974) AND 2:40 (less than a year later). More importantly, she served as a spokeswoman for the successful effort to put this event on the international calendar.

## ❏ JACQUELINE HANSEN

Topanga, California. Born November 20th, 1948, in Binghamton, New York. 5'3", 108 pounds. Married, one child. Occupation: track and cross country coach. Began racing in 1966. Runs for San Fernando Valley Track Club. Coach: Laszlo Tabori.

## ❏ BEST TIMES

1500, 4:28; 3000, 9:55; 10-K, 34:50; 15-K, 52:51; marathon, 2:38:19.

## ❏ TRAINING PLAN

Since 1970, I've basically trained on intervals.

## ❏ SAMPLE WEEK

Shortly before 2:38:19 marathon in 1975.

Monday—A.M., five-lap warmup; 20 laps including 100 and 150 intervals. P.M., nine miles.

Tuesday, P.M., 2½-mile warmup; 15 x 100, eight medium, seven hard; 10 x 400 with three hard (73, 71, 72 seconds); 2½ laps easy; 8 x 150, two medium, one hard; five laps hard (5:13 mile); two laps easy; five laps hard (5:17 mile);

2½ laps easy; 10 x 200, two hard, two medium; two laps easy; 12 x 100, two medium, one hard.

Wednesday—A.M., five-lap warmup; 20 laps, usual sets of intervals. P.M., eight miles.

Thursday—A.M., four miles easy. P.M., 2½-mile warmup; 10 x 100, six medium, four hard; 4 x 250, two hard, one easy, one hard; 800 hard (2:24); 6 x 150, one hard, one medium; 2½ laps easy; 3 x 250 buildups; two laps easy; 10 x 100; 2 x 200 hard.

Friday—P.M., three miles and 12 x 100.

Saturday—5-K cross country race in 16:55.

Sunday—19 miles.

## ❏ FAVORITE WORKOUT

I always loved my 25-lappers: warm up five laps and continue to run 20 more with various sets of sprinting straightaways and jogging curves. For example, 2 x 100 medium, 2 x 150 hard, 2 x 100 medium, 2 x 100 hard. Valuable for endurance and speed, and can easily be run alone, anywhere.

# DAN HELD

■ *The most competitive international road races aren't marathons. Injuries, voluntary absences, dropouts and (usually) heat diminish Olympic and World Championships. World Half-Marathons generally draw better fields and produce better performances. Dan Held has been there twice, and in 1994 led the U.S. team's finishers.*

❏ **DANIEL HELD**

Waukesha, Wisconsin. Born October 15th, 1965, in Milwaukee, Wisconsin. 5'9", 138 pounds. Married, no children. Occupation: claims adjuster. Began racing in 1980. Runs for Nike. Self-coached.

❏ **BEST TIMES**

Track 5000, 13:41; 8-K, 23:09; 10-K, 28:56; 10 miles, 47:54; half-marathon, 1:02:46; marathon, 2:13:50.

❏ **TRAINING PLAN**

My general approach is to use strength as the main emphasis; I believe that strength IS speed. I am a high-mileage runner— 100 to 120 average, higher in marathon buildups. I have two buildup phases—January through March, then race March to June; take a break for two weeks, then repeat buildup July through September, and race from August to November or December.

❏ **SAMPLE WEEK**

Of 125 to 130 miles.

Sunday—20-25 miles, hilly terrain, averaging 5:45 pace.

Monday—A.M., eight miles. P.M., 5 x mile in 4:30-4:35 or 4 x 2000 at same pace as miles; 12-14 miles total.

Tuesday—A.M., eight miles. P.M., 10 miles.

Wednesday—A.M., eight miles. P.M., 10 miles.

Thursday—A.M., eight miles easy. P.M., 10 x hill repeats (five on 300-meter hill, five on 100-meter); 11 miles total.

Friday—A.M., six miles easy. P.M., eight miles easy.

Saturday—either 15-mile uptempo run over hilly course (surging hills), or 12-16 x 400 on track at 65-second pace.

## ❏ FAVORITE WORKOUT

Mile repeats—especially on cross country terrain. It's a necessary fitness builder but also a great confidence booster. When I do this workout, I get pretty fired up to compete.

# HAL HIGDON

*Higdon practically invented modern running writing. He wrote professionally before most of today's writers had mastered their spelling, phonics and penmanship—or had even begun fingerpainting in preschool. Higdon backs his words with racing accomplishments as diverse as a fifth-place Boston Marathon finish (in 1964) and an American masters steeplechase record that still stands two decades later.*

## ❏ HAL HIGDON

Michigan City, Indiana. Born June 17th, 1931, in Chicago, Illinois. 5'10", 142 pounds. Married, three children, six grandchildren. Occupation: writer. Began racing in 1947. Runs for Dunes Running Club. Self-coached.

## ❏ BEST TIMES

Mile, 4:13.6; 3000 steeplechase, 9:13.8 (9:18.6 as master); 5000, 14:43.6 (14:59.6 as master); 10,000, 31:06.5 (31:08 as master); marathon, 2:21:55 (2:29:27 as master).

## ❏ TRAINING PLAN

I follow the hard-easy approach—not only day by day, but in weeks, months and even years. I regularly change my training focus and experiment with new methods, as my mood changes and to test new approaches for the readers of *Runner's World*.

## ❏ SAMPLE WEEK

Of 39 miles from October 1994.

Sunday—one-hour 20-minute trail run in Indiana Dunes State

Park, very hilly, loose footing.

Monday—A.M., easy 56-minute run on golf course. P.M., running in water at beach.

Tuesday—10 x 1-K on cross country course, walk three minutes between.

Wednesday—easy three miles.

Thursday—rest.

Friday—12 miles on road, good pace.

Saturday—three miles miscellaneous running while watching high school cross country meet.

❑ FAVORITE WORKOUT.

Tempo run on trail (usually flat trail at Indiana Dunes State Park). Start easy (15 to 20 minutes), then accelerate to race pace (20 to 30 minutes), then back to easy (10 to 15 minutes). Refreshing mentally, develops anaerobic power and form.

# RON HILL

■ *Hill is a research chemist by training, but he could have been a mathematician. He loves his numbers, and they add up impressively. Hill included a note with his questionnaire, reporting that in mid-1995 he'd run more than 30 years without missing a day . . . was about to pass his 130,000th recorded mile in 39 years of log-keeping. . . and was aiming for his 2000th race before turning 60. More numbers he didn't mention: three-time British Olympian; world record-setter at three track distances (10 miles, 15 miles and 25-K), and second man below 2:10 in the marathon.*

❏ **RONALD HILL**

Hyde, England. Born September 25th, 1938, in Accrington, England. 5'6½", 126 pounds. Married, two children. Occupation: sports textiles consultant. Began racing in 1954. Runs for Clayton-le-Moors Harriers. Self-coached.

❏ **BEST TIMES**

Mile, 4:10.1; three miles, 13:27.2; six miles, 27:26.0; 10,000, 28:39.2; marathon, 2:09:28.

❏ **TRAINING PLAN**

For marathon, worked on a 10-week schedule, gradually building distance and amount of speedwork for six weeks. After a major marathon, four weeks of active "rest" with 30, 40, 50 and 50 miles easy running.

❏ **SAMPLE WEEK**

In June-July 1970, four weeks before 2:09:28 marathon; 140 miles for the week.

**Ron Hill in his heyday: 1970 European
Championships marathon winner.**

Saturday—A.M., 7.5 miles easy. P.M., 13.5 miles, bursts or fartlek on all uphills.

Sunday—28 miles easy with Arthur Walsham on very hilly course.

Monday—A.M., 7.5 miles easy. P.M., 10 miles including 2 x 2-minute and 20 x 30-second strides.

Tuesday—A.M., 7.5 miles easy. Noon, 1.5-mile warmup; 2 x 400 in 58.8 and 57.9; P.M., eight miles easy.

Wednesday—A.M., 7.5 miles easy. P.M., 12 miles with four miles of fartlek.

Thursday—A.M., 7.5 miles easy. Noon, six miles easy. P.M., eight miles easy.

Friday—A.M., 7.5 miles easy. P.M., seven miles easy.

## ❏ FAVORITE WORKOUT

I live in a hilly district and like to include bursts/fartlek on all uphills. This builds strength and speed in an informal session.

# SISTER MARION IRVINE

*That's Sister, as in Catholic nun. Through her younger years, she hid her excess weight under the traditional habit. She also smoked to excess. Running didn't start until her late 40s. That story continues in the sidebar.*

❏ **MARION IRVINE**

Santa Rosa, California. Born October 19th, 1929, in San Francisco, California. 5'10", 132 pounds. Occupation: educator. Began racing in 1978. Runs for Tamalpa Runners. Coach: Kees Tuinzing.

❏ **BEST TIMES**

5-K, 18:28; 8-K, 30:31; 10-K, 37:43; 15-K, 57:52; 10 miles, 1:02:58; 20-K, 1:26:24; half-marathon, 1:23:16; 20 miles, 2:12:24; marathon, 2:51:01.

❏ **TRAINING PLAN**

Now that I no longer compete, I cross-train—hiking, swimming, cycling, weights, road and track running.

❏ **SAMPLE WEEK**

From June 1995.

Sunday—bike 30-K; hike 3.5 miles; swim half-mile.

Monday—run on track, 5 x 100, 2 x 80, 2 x 50, 6 x 50, 10 x 80, 6 x 300, 1 x 800; hike four miles.

Tuesday—swim one mile; hike 12-K.

Wednesday—hike 10-K; swim one mile.

Thursday—run on track, 1 x mile, 5 x 150, 4 x 300, 1 x mile.

Friday—hike 10-K; swim 1-K.

Saturday—hike 10-K.

## ❏ FAVORITE WORKOUT

No particular favorite anymore; I stay active every day I can.

# NUN BETTER

August 1989 *Running Commentary*

To this six-year-old girl, no one at the mountain resort's swimming pool was a stranger. She talked with anyone who would talk back.

When a woman with curly gray hair stood up to leave, the little girl demanded to know, "Where are you going?" "To run," said the woman. "Run?" the girl said. "Young people run. Old ones JOG."

"How old do you think I am?" asked the tall, lean woman. "Sixty," the girl guessed, almost correctly. Marion Irvine—Sister Marion, the Catholic nun of 1984 Olympic Trials fame—would turn 60 in October. This fact distresses her, not because she's getting older but because she was barely too young for a new age group at the recent World Veterans Championships.

Sister Marion laughs when she recalls talking with the six-year-old at Jeff Galloway's Lake Tahoe running camp this summer. "She knew better than I what I should do."

Irvine never was a jogger. Almost at once, she went from obesity and two-pack-a-day smoking to racing.

That was 11 years, many successes and one big setback ago. After discovering racing, she indulged often. "I loved three-day holiday weekends," she says, "because I could race on Saturday, Sunday and Monday."

Even when running alone, she raced herself. Her training plan: "Always run as far as possible, as fast as possible."

Marion ran 16 marathons in four years. In late 1983, she qualified for the Trials with 2:51:01. At Olympia, she ran 2:52:02. She was

54 then. No one that age has yet run faster.

But neither has Irvine herself tried another marathon since 1984. Her biggest setback immediately followed her greatest success. "I thought I was invincible after the Trial," she says. "I started training hard again the next day and tried for a 10-K PR two weeks later." During that race, she suddenly thought, "I'm not enjoying this." Finding no ready reason to go on, she dropped out.

Guilt quickly replaced her weariness. "I began berating myself," she remembers. "I told myself I wasn't a quitter."

The way to prove it was jump in her car and drive to another race the same day. She finished that one, but two days later suffered a hamstring tear. Its after-effects lasted for almost three years.

You don't really become a runner until you've had a serious, career-threatening injury. It makes you appreciate what you had and examine what went wrong. "I've become a runner," says Irvine.

"I saw that if I intended to be competing in the 95-plus age group, I needed to be better balanced in my running. "I made a bargain with God: Just get me through this [injury], and I'll do things right next time." She still trains and races hard, just not as often. She races less than before, subscribes to the hard/easy system, and limits herself to one long run, one in hills and one session of intervals a week.

Marion doesn't race as fast as before, or as far. But she says, "I'm just so happy to be out there running without pain." Today's pains most often come from non-running causes, but hurt no less for that. In one incredible streak of bad luck this winter and spring, she: (1) dislocated a thumb, (2) spent nine weeks with the flu; (3) tripped and fell on a shoulder; (4) broke a toe, and (5) bruised and cut her face in a bike wreck.

Still, Sister Marion ran the World Veterans Championships for the third straight time. Despite being oldest in her age group, she won five gold medals. She skipped the distance that made her famous. "I can now enter 10-K's, run three or four minutes slower than my PR and be satisfied," she says. "I can't do that in the marathon. I still think of myself as top-class in that event, and can't yet imagine going to a race, running 3:25 or 3:30, and having people ask what was wrong. I know I finally will have arrived as a runner when I can run a marathon just to finish and be happy with that."

(Sister Marion still hasn't returned to marathoning. But she continues to run, and bike, and swim, and row in her late 60s.)

# JULIE ISPHORDING

> It was all new in 1984—new for women who were running their first Olympic Marathon Trial, and new for Isphording who made the original U.S. team as its youngest member at 22. This was before the injuries that interfered with her race at the Games and often interrupted a still-brilliant career. It has including victories at the Los Angeles and Columbus Marathons, and an appearance at the first Goodwill Games.

## ❏ JULIE ISPHORDING

Cincinnati, Ohio. Born December 5th, 1961, in Cincinnati. 5'5", 108 pounds. Single. Occupation: marketing director. Began racing in 1979. Coach: Pete Pfitzinger.

## ❏ BEST TIMES

10-K, 33:21. Marathon, 2:30:54.

## ❏ TRAINING PLAN

Key elements have always been long runs, speed and hills-- and fun! However, because of my many injuries, I can't do the high mileage I love and believe in. Hill repeats are bad for me, too. Pete Pfitzinger is one of the most knowledgeable and supportive coaches I know, and a great friend I depend on a lot.

## ❏ SAMPLE WEEK

From 1995, after 2½ years off with injuries; week's mileage, 64, plus stationary biking and swimming.

Sunday—easy 10 miles.

Monday—eight miles, hilly, at 6:50 pace.

Tuesday—four-mile warmup; 15 laps of fast straights, jog curves; four-mile warmdown.

Wednesday—no running.

Thursday—four-mile warmup; 6 x 800; four-mile warmdown.

Friday—8.5 miles at 6:45 pace, hilly course.

Saturday—15 miles at 6:50 pace.

## ❏ FAVORITE WORKOUT

Long run with friends. (Hate track workouts and try to avoid them!)

Janeart, Ltd.

**Julie Isphording**

# JEFF JACOBS

It's short-sighted to look at the dearth of sub-2:10 American marathoners (only two since 1983) and think this country doesn't produce good runners anymore. It's wrong to overlook the flock of sub-2:15 runners with the potential to break through. Few of them sport a finer resume' than Jacobs, who has broken 4:00 in a mile and flirted with 28:00 in a 10-K.

❏ JEFFREY P. JACOBS

Roscoe, Illinois. Born June 29th, 1964, in Clinton, Iowa. 6'1", 156 pounds. Married, three children. Occupation: engineer. Began racing in 1979. Runs for Nike. Coach: Bud James.

❏ BEST TIMES

1500, 3:43 (1986); mile, 3:58 (1991); 3000, 8:05 (1986); 5000, 13:46 (1991); 8-K, 22:44 (1991); track 10,000, 28:37 (1992); road 10-K, 28:08 (1991); 10 miles, 47:45 (1994); half-marathon, 1:03:42 (1993); marathon, 2:13:44 (1994).

❏ TRAINING PLAN

In the winter, I do strength-type workouts. As the spring approaches, I work on speed-strength combination workouts. I tend to avoid the track and do my workouts either on the road or a marked bike path.

❏ SAMPLE WEEK

Of 101 miles before a marathon. For non-marathon training, I don't do the five-mile morning runs and average 75 to 80 miles a week.

Sunday—six miles easy, usually at 6:00 pace.

Monday—A.M., 10 miles at 5:40-6:00 pace. P.M., half-mile warmup, four-mile stepdown (5:15, 5:00, 4:45, 4:25), half-mile cooldown.

Tuesday—A.M., five miles at 6:00 pace. P.M., 10 miles at 6:00 pace.

Wednesday—A.M., five miles at 6:00 pace. P.M., two-mile warmup, 10 x 800 at 2:10 with 400 jog between, two-mile cooldown.

Thursday—A.M., five miles at 6:00 pace. P.M., 10 miles at 6:00 pace.

Friday—A.M., five miles at 6:00 pace. P.M., 10 miles with 6-8 75-second surges, 90 seconds between.

Saturday—20-22 miles at 5:40-6:00 pace.

## ❏ FAVORITE WORKOUT

I like the Monday stepdown four-mile because it is a good indicator of my conditioning. If I can run the first three miles under 5:00-4:50-4:40 and the last mile sub-4:30, I know I am fit.

# DON JANICKI

*Conventional wisdom now proclaims that young runners must avoid marathons. Too damaging to the legs and speed. Too risky to the runner's longevity. The critics haven't talked with Janicki, who ran his first marathon as a high schooler. . . then enjoyed a successful college career at shorter distances. . . then PRed at 2:11 more than a dozen years after becoming a marathoner.*

## ❏ DONALD P. JANICKI

Louisville, Colorado. Born April 30th, 1960, in Sacramento, California. 5'10", 139 pounds. Married, three children. Occupation: association account manager. Began racing in 1976. Runs for New Balance. Self-coached.

## ❏ BEST TIMES

Track 5000, 13:44; track 10,000, 28:27; road 10-K, 27:56; 15-K, 43:58; half-marathon, 1:03:15; marathon, 2:11:16.

## ❏ TRAINING PLAN

Basically, I use the hard-easy method with long intervals, short intervals and a long run as the hard workouts. I usually do two marathons a year and use the following schedule for 10 weeks before.

## ❏ SAMPLE WEEK

Of 100 to 110 miles.

Sunday—A.M., 20-23 miles at 6:30 pace, picking up toward the end to 5:30-6:00. P.M., sometimes an easy four miles.

Monday—A.M., five miles and weights. P.M., seven miles.

**Don Janicki**

Tuesday—A.M., 5-7 miles. P.M., long intervals (6 x 1600 or 8 x 1000).

Wednesday—A.M., five miles and weights. P.M., seven miles.

Thursday—A.M., 12-15 miles. P.M., 5-8 miles.

Friday—A.M., five miles and weights. P.M., short intervals (12 x 400 or 8 x 800).

Saturday—A.M., 7-10 miles easy. P.M., 4-5 miles easy or rest.

## ❏ FAVORITE WORKOUTS

(1) Repeat miles at 10-K race pace with 400 between. (2) Long runs at a quick pace.

# LYNN JENNINGS

No woman runner—anywhere in the world, at any time—
sports a more complete racing bio than Jennings. Pick any
type of running, and she has mastered it. Outdoor track:
Olympic medalist and American record-holder in the
10,000. Cross country: three-time winner at the World
Championships. Indoor track: two World medals in the
3000. Road racing gets the least of her attention, yet she
has run a world-best time in the 8-K and an American
record for 10-K. She might apply her considerable skills to
the marathon when her track work is complete. See the
sidebar for more of Jennings' story.

## ❏ LYNN JENNINGS

Newmarket, New Hampshire. Born July 1st, 1960, in Princeton,
New Jersey. 5'5", 110 pounds. Married. Occupation: athlete.
Began racing in 1975 at age 14. Runs for Nike International.
Coach: John Babington.

## ❏ BEST TIMES

1500, 4:06; mile, 4:24; 3000, 8:40; 5000 (track), 15:07; 5-K (road),
15:12; 8-K, 25:02; 10,000 (track), 31:19; 10-K (road), 31:06.

## ❏ TRAINING PLAN

I am not an overmileage fanatic—85 per week tops. And I am
not an overracing geek. I plot my seasons very carefully, yet
I'm a year-round racer—cross country, indoor, outdoor track,
roads.

## ❏ SAMPLE WEEK

When not racing, I run 70 to 85 miles as follows:

Sunday—long run, 14 to 15 miles hilly at about 6:15 pace.

Monday—two runs totaling 10 to 15 miles.

Tuesday—easy run in morning, track session in afternoon.

Wednesday—two runs totaling 10 to 15 miles.

Thursday—two runs totaling 10 to 20 miles at brisk pace.

Friday—easy run in morning, track session in afternoon.

Saturday—two runs totaling 10 to 15 miles.

I run easily the two days before a race. Yet I still do a track session four days before a big event—even the Olympics.

## ❏ FAVORITE WORKOUT

Any track session devised by John Babington. I know it will cover the bases and have several long-lasting benefits.

# LOOKING UP TO LYNN

"Who are your early heroes?" asked John Cobley of *British Columbia Athletics Report* in a recent interview. Naming the runners I'd once idolized was easy, even 30 years later.

Then Cobley asked, "Who are your current heroes?" That question didn't have a ready answer.

I've run out of heroes. Idolizing someone young enough to be my child would be silly, but I'm not too old to play favorites.

Lynn Jennings makes the short list of most-admired athletes. She's a runner for all seasons: world champion in cross-country, Olympian in outdoor track, American record holder indoors, and owner of world and U.S. road marks.

Jennings' versatility and year-round consistency is unmatched. But a runner needs more than talent to become a favorite. Lynn has more.

She gives you a firm handshake, looks you in the eye, calls you by name and says what she thinks. She also takes commitments seriously.

Jennings committed herself last year to run the National Women's 8-K Championship in Alhambra, California, but couldn't go because of an ankle sprain. She promised then to be there in 1991, and was.

Before racing, she gave a clinic for the area's high school runners. She admitted her failures: running herself into knee surgery in high school and retiring three times while still young.

In her mid-20s, Jennings decided, "I was born to be a runner.

When I told that to my parents, they supported my decision but weren't thrilled. I could see Dad thinking he had just spent $40,000 on my Princeton education so I could run around in sneakers the rest of my life."

Lynn also wasn't shy about telling her strengths. "I'm one of the wiser runners out there on the circuit," she said. "I never ignore what my body tells me, and I never get overuse injuries."

Yet she confessed to pushing nearer the edge this year than ever before. She overtrained before the Worlds and ran one of her worst races at the New York Games in July.

She had to run two sub-32-minute 10,000s within five days in Tokyo. Then she married Dave Hill and traveled to Barcelona for a preview of the Olympic site.

The Alhambra 8-K would be her third road race in less than three weeks, a far busier schedule than Jennings prefers. But she made no excuses about feeling tired or this being her down-season. She wasn't coy about her intentions.

Lynn said, "I want to break 25:02. That's the existing world record [which she held]. I've been thinking about that for a couple of months.

"I'm not thinking I MIGHT be able to do it. I'm thinking I WILL do it."

But records can't be scheduled, even by the most determined runners and generous sponsors. They can't order perfect conditions.

The weather this last Saturday in October turned un-Californian. After five years of drought, heavy rains suddenly blew through Alhambra.

The rain could have improved Jennings' chances if it had simply cooled the temperature and cleared out the smog. But the storm also brought wind, a headwind for the return leg of the out-and-back course.

**Lynn Jennings**

Lynn might have given up her record attempt before it started. Instead, she raced to the halfway mark 19 seconds faster than record pace before turning into the wind.

It slowed her to 25:23. Not a record but an admirable try by an admirable runner.

(The next year, Jennings became the first American woman to win an Olympic medal at any track distance longer than 800 meters with her bronze in the 10,000. She now has won three World Cross Countries and medaled twice at the World Indoor Championships.)

# DON KARDONG

*His books and* Runner's World *articles make us smile, if not laugh out loud. But humorist Kardong also has a serious side. Without one, you don't almost medal at the Olympics (three seconds shy of bronze in the Montreal Marathon), found one of the country's largest road races (Lilac Bloomsday), stabilize professional racing (as he did as longtime president of ARRA) and lead the country's long distance runners (as a TAC chairman). Kardong couldn't resist adding to his reply: "It's tough to stare one's younger, fitter self in the face. Where did that guy go? I'm now one-sixth heavier, half as well trained and injured three times as often!"*

## ❑ DONALD FRANKLIN KARDONG

Spokane, Washington. Born December 22nd, 1948, in Kirkland, Washington. 6'3", 150 pounds. Married, two children. Occupation: writer and consultant (teacher at time of best racing). Began racing in 1964. Ran for Club Northwest. Coaches: Marshall Clark at Stanford, Tracy Walters in 1976.

## ❑ BEST TIMES

Mile, 4:01.9 (1974); three miles, 12:57.6 (1974); marathon, 2:11:16 (1976).

## ❑ TRAINING PLAN

In my best training years (about 1974-76), I trained as a 5000-meter runner. I ran intervals twice and sometimes three times a week. Most were in the 200- to 1200-meter range. I also thrived on high mileage, generally 100 to 110 miles a week). Summers and winters were relaxed.

**Don Kardong leads the 1976 Olympic Trials 5000m.**

## ❏ SAMPLE WEEK

Of 109.5 miles, about a month before three-mile PR in 1974.

Sunday—16 miles, steady pace.

Monday—A.M., five miles. P.M., two-mile warmup; track workout with four sets of 6 x 300, 48-49 seconds, 100 recovery jog; two-mile cooldown; 10.5 miles total.

Tuesday—A.M., five miles. P.M., 10 miles steady.

Wednesday—A.M., five miles. P.M., 10 miles steady.

Thursday—A.M., five miles. P.M., road fartlek with three sets of two minutes-one minute-30 seconds, then four minutes, then two more sets of two minutes-one minute-30 seconds; 10 miles total.

Friday—A.M., five miles. P.M., 12 miles steady.

Saturday—A.M., five miles steady. P.M., 10 miles steady.

## ❏ FAVORITE WORKOUT

The type shown on Thursday P.M. It was intense, combined short and long intervals, but was less tedious than similar work on the track since it was untimed.

# JOHN A. KELLEY

> *It's no contest. He is the all-time Mr. Running USA. This honor goes to him not just for what he did while young— two Boston Marathon titles, 10 years apart, plus three Olympic teams—but for what he kept doing well into his 80s. Kelley counts 61 Boston Marathons among more than 1000 lifetime races.*

## ❏ JOHN A. KELLEY

East Dennis, Massachusetts. Born September 6th, 1907, in West Medford, Massachusetts. 5'6", 128 pounds. Retired. Widowed. Began racing in 1928. Runs for Cape Cod Athletic Club. Self-coached.

## ❏ BEST TIME

Marathon, 2:30:45 (1945).

## ❏ TRAINING PLAN

At the time Kelley was surveyed, he was coping with the death of his wife. He suggested merely selecting comments from his biography, *Young at Heart* (WRS Publishing, 1992).

On being coached: "Clarence DeMar [seven-time Boston winner] used to say, 'Self-directed work is play,' and that's true. That's why I've always coached myself."

On training in his prime: "Years ago, we just ran anything. There was no set program, no schedule. We just ran to enjoy it. I averaged 35 or 40 miles a week. I don't think I ever ran over 60 miles a week in my life. I'd always run three or four days a week."

**Johnny Kelley**

On running by time: "I ran on the watch, never on miles. If you said to go out and run 15 or 20 miles, it would scare me. But two hours or an hour—I've always trained that way."

On his training now: " 'Train sane,' that's my motto. All these runners that do 120 miles a week, they eventually run into trouble. Jeepers, they run every day. I believe that if you're tired, you should take a day off."

On cross-training: "I try to do something every day [if not running], whether walking or swimming."

On his Boston training in later years: "I started to get ready after Christmas by adding long workouts [up from his usual hour]. I took a long run every two or three weeks—the longest 2½ hours the end of March, then coasting to conserve energy for my big push."

On his 61 Boston starts and 58 finishes: "I didn't try to set this record, you know. It just happened. But if anyone ever does break my record, I'd love to shake his hand."

# JOHN J. KELLEY

■ *"The Younger Kelley," the sidebar calls him. He's passing through his 60s now but will always be junior to unrelated John A. Kelley. John J. broke an 12-year drought of American winners at the 1957 Boston Marathon, and almost broke 2:20 at a time when Americans seldom cracked 2:30.*

## ❏ JOHN J. KELLEY

Mystic, Connecticut. Born December 24th, 1930, in Norwich, Connecticut. 5'6", 125 pounds. Married, three children. Occupation: teacher and writer. Began racing in 1946. Runs for Boston Athletic Association. Coached by Johnny Semple (deceased).

## ❏ BEST TIME

Marathon, 2:20:05 (1957).

## ❏ TRAINING PLAN

Long runs at varied speeds over varied terrain—anywhere, but preferably "escaping" (from human congestion) by running on paths. Typical week in the late 1950s and early '60s totaled 85 to 98 miles.

## ❏ SAMPLE WEEK

Of 80 miles, about a month before winning 1957 Boston Marathon.

Sunday—16 miles, including 15 x 220 yards in 35 seconds between miles nine and 13; total time 1:42.

Monday—seven miles in 50 minutes.

Tuesday—A.M., 11 miles in 1:17. P.M., six miles in 43 minutes.

Wednesday—10+ miles in 1:08.

Thursday—8+ miles in 55 minutes, including 2 x 440 yards in 65 seconds at six and 7-3/4 miles.

Friday—four miles in 28 minutes.

Saturday—30-K race in 1:44.

## ❏ FAVORITE WORKOUT

My best was a mix of distance and speed, covering 12 to 16 miles and involving what later came to be called "ladder" intervals, usually on the watch—75 seconds with 75-second jog, 2:30 fast, 2:30 rest, etc.

# THE YOUNGER KELLEY

Old Johnny Kelley has run the last of his 61 Boston Marathons. You might wonder who'll replace him as the one person who best lives its history.

Old John took over that role from Clarence DeMar, who ran the race from its 14th to 58th years. Who'll pick up the torch now?

No one else needs to apply as torchbearer. Boston already has filled Johnny Kelley's position—with another Johnny Kelley.

John Adelbert Kelley, born 1907, and John Joseph Kelley, born 1930, are related only by what they've done at the Boston Marathon. John A. did more here than his namesake, so he was always more the media's darling.

Old John won Boston twice, Young John once. Old John placed second here seven times, Young John five. Old John ran about twice as many Bostons as Young John has run so far.

Still, the two Kelleys were at least equals outside of Boston. Each competed in two Olympics, where their placings were almost identical.

Young John won eight national marathon titles in a row between 1956 and '63. He came within six seconds of being the first American to break 2:20.

This Kelley, not the older one, was my earliest running hero. I told in a *Runner's World* column about meeting him for the first time, describing him as "a scale-model John Kennedy in both appearance and accent. Kelley spoke modestly but well about his running then and now. I knew I had picked the right hero all those years ago."

He became heroic for the most superficial of reasons: He was my size but much faster. Tom Derderian's book, *Boston Marathon*, showed that Kelley and I were more alike than I'd known.

Kelley made a break from his college coach, as I did later with mine. "The Boston University coach saw no future in running long, slow distances instead of rapid quarter-miles," writes Derderian. "But Kelley saw no future in endless quarter-miles."

He preferred road racing, as I did. He found the same magic in words.

"Kelley read too much and thought too much," says Derderian. "He studied literature. He wrote, and wrote well."

Derderian describes the younger Kelley as "Henry David Thoreau at six minutes a mile. . . He accepted inspiration but did not wait to be told what to do. Nor did he like being told what to do.

"This was a generation of running rebels." It predated mine by more than a decade.

Kelley made a career of teaching high school English and coaching runners. At age 63, he has run the Boston Marathon more than 30 times (most recently with an injury-slowed 4:07 finish in 1992, but he was still flirting with three hours in his mid-50s).

"I run with no conscious desire to fill Johnny A.'s shoes," says Johnny J. Yet he reaches further back into Boston's storied history than anyone now running here.

(The line of succession at Boston runs long and strong. John J. Kelley's 1957 win was the first by an American since John A.'s 12 years earlier. Amby Burfoot, in 1968, was the first U.S. winner since John J., who was Burfoot's coach. Burfoot was a college roommate and early mentor of four-time Boston winner Bill Rodgers.)

# JOHN KESTON

*Running life began at 55 for Keston. At the time, he'd already traveled widely as a professional singer and actor. But racing let him explore even more of the world—and break many world age-group records. He is, at this writing, the oldest sub-three-hour marathoner. Keston ran 2:58:32 as a 69-year-old, then at 70 set records at distances as short as one mile.*

## ❏ JOHN KESTON

McMinnville, Oregon. Born December 5th, 1924, in London, England. 6'0", 150 pounds. Married, six children, nine grandchildren. Occupation: actor-singer, retired university professor. Began racing in 1980. Runs for Oregon Road Runners Club. Self-coached.

## ❏ BEST TIMES

Since age 65. 1500, 5:09 (1992); road mile, 5:21 (1993); track mile, 5:33 (1992); 3000, 10:51 (1995); two miles, 11:57 (1993); 5-K, 18:22 (1991); 8-K, 30:07 (1992); 10-K, 36:34 (1991); 12-K, 46:52 (1994); 15-K, 58:02 (1994); 10 miles, 1:03:08 (1992); half-marathon, 1:23:16 (1991); 25-K, 1:42:09 (1991); marathon, 2:58:13 (1991).

## ❏ TRAINING PLAN

I haven't consciously trained for any specific season. I've usually tried to do some speedwork weekly, and a long run or two (10 to 15 miles and longer) each week. Between 1985 and '88, I did train specifically for marathons. I used Jeff Galloway's schedule with a long run every three weeks and mile intervals every two weeks (building up to 13 x mile).

## ❏ SAMPLE WEEK

Of 55 miles from 1991.

Sunday—88-minute run through woods at eight-minute pace.

Monday—seven miles on road and trails at sub-seven-minute pace.

Tuesday—two-mile warmup; three miles of fartlek on blacktop roads; 10 x 100-plus meters between telephone poles, flat out; three-mile cooldown.

Wednesday—easy run at faster than normal training pace, 7:00-7:15; stopped to stretch four times.

Thursday—five miles easy, but couldn't resist running mile four in 6:56.

Friday—three miles very easy; three hours of upper-body work, throwing gravel for parking area.

Saturday—mile warmup; 10-K cross country race in 39:07 at Lake George, Minnesota; mile cooldown.

## ❏ FAVORITE WORKOUT

Long run, 10 to 15 miles, with six or seven one-mile intervals at 90 percent of 10-K race pace. I like this workout because I don't take too much out of myself and recovery quickly.

# SANDY KIDDY

Dr. Joan Ullyot (profiled later in this book) once wrote that we get about 10 years racing improvement, regardless of starting age. Kiddy began racing two weeks after turning 40, and in her fastest decade she ran a 2:53 marathon and 15:12 for 100 miles. But she didn't suddenly fall apart when the warranty expired. Running in the World 100-K at 55, she became the oldest American ever to make a national all-ages team in any event.

## ❑ SANDRA JEAN KIDDY

Palm Springs, California. Born November 27th, 1936, in Grand Rapids, Michigan. 5'2", 105 pounds. Married, one child. Occupation: retired. Began racing in 1976. Self-coached.

## ❑ BEST TIMES

10-K, 38:24 (1982); 15-K, 58:50 (1982); half-marathon, 1:25:15 (1983); 30-K, 2:05:30 (1983); marathon, 2:53:23 (1982); 50-K, 3:32:34 (1983); 50 miles, 6:09:09 (1984); 100-K, 7:49:20 (1984); 100 miles, 15:12:54 (1985).

## ❑ TRAINING PLAN

I tried to run 80 or more miles per week with one to three bursts of speed in each run, plus the hill workout listed below as my favorite. I used shorter races as training runs for longer-distance racing goals. Before my best marathon, I ran races of half-marathon, 10-K and 15-K in immediate consecutive weekends. In the month before my best 100-K race, I ran a 36.2-mile race, a marathon and a 15-K.

## ❑ SAMPLE WEEK

Of 69.7 miles before best marathon, with all training that

week on flat roads.

Sunday—half-marathon race in 1:26:04.

Monday—10 miles in 1:18:26

Tuesday—12.4 miles in 1:37:06

Wednesday—9.5 miles in 1:15:21

Thursday—12.5 miles in 1:34:02

Friday—six miles in 52:08

Saturday—10-K race in 38:50.

❏ **FAVORITE WORKOUT**

Tram run: 1.75-mile warmup to road leading to Palm Springs tram station, then up from 500 feet to 2500 feet elevation in four miles, and return by same route. Because of the warm to very hot weather in Palm Springs, we did no speedwork, only this workout about once a week.

# JANIS KLECKER

*Notice how Klecker lists her occupations below. First comes mother, then dentist, and only then runner. This is her order of priorities. She already was practicing dentistry as Dr. Klecker when she won the 1992 Olympic Marathon Trial and placed 20th at the Barcelona Games. Then she and husband Barney started their family with twins, and their third child was born two years later. She had no problem letting them put her other career options on hold.*

## ❏ JANIS K. KLECKER

Minnetonka, Minnesota. Born July 18th, 1960, in Minnesota. 5'6", 115 pounds. Married, three children. Occupation: mother, dentist, runner. Began racing in 1979 at age 18. Runs for Asics. Coach: Barney Klecker.

## ❏ BEST TIMES

5-K, 15:59 (1992); 8-K, 25:53 (1990); 10-K, 31:44 (1990); 10 miles, 53:35 (1992); half-marathon, 1:10:41 (1990); marathon, 2:30:12 (1992); 50-K, 3:13:51 (1983).

## ❏ TRAINING PLAN

I run 65 to 90 miles a week, and include hill-interval training, long runs and easy days. I do a fair amount of training on a treadmill. I also cross-train quite a bit—stationary bike ride, stair machine, Nordic Track, weight training, swimming and Aquajogging.

## ❏ SAMPLE WEEK

My training varies a lot due to family obligations and what specific racing I am training for. This very general schedule adds us to 65 to 90 miles of running per week, plus cross-

**Janis Klecker, after her triumph at the 1992 Olympic Trials marathon.**

training:

Sunday—six miles.

Monday—eight half-mile hill repeats or treadmill.

Tuesday—six to eight miles.

Wednesday—15 miles at good pace.

Thursday—half-mile to mile repeats, four to six of them.

Friday—six to 10 miles easy.

Saturday—20 to 24 miles.

## ❏ FAVORITE WORKOUT

Long run of 18 to 24 miles. I enjoy the time alone, and I feel it gives me confidence for racing.

# INGRID KRISTIANSEN

*In spring 1985, we didn't yet know how great Ingrid Kristiansen would become. She was still "the other Norwegian," behind Grete Waitz. That year, when Kristiansen set a world marathon record of 2:21:06 at London, we didn't think it would last. Later in 1985, Joan Samuelson came within 15 seconds of the record at Chicago—while beating Ingrid. But, at this writing, Kristiansen remains the record holder. Her mark, now one of the oldest in the sport, looks better all the time. She also held the 5000 and 10,000 records until the mid-1990s.*

## ❑ INGRID KRISTIANSEN

Oslo, Norway. Born March 21st, 1956, in Trondheim, Norway. 5'6", 110 pounds. Married, three children, ages 12, five and two. Began competing as a cross-country skier in 1966, and as a runner in 1972. Coach: Johan Kaggestad.

## ❑ BEST TIMES

1500, 4:05.97; 3000, 8:34.10; 5000, 14:37.33; 10,000, 30:13.74; half-marathon, 1:06:40; marathon, 2:21:06.

## ❑ TRAINING PLAN

I base my training philosophy on the holistic approach. This means that your focus has to be very broad, your lifestyle around the clock has to be good. An athlete should not be an athlete only two or three hours a day, but 24 hours a day.

People I see failing as runners do not necessarily fail in their training. They fail because they are not managing their life. Simple things like diversity in interests, friends and family, how you manage success and failure, how you control the

**Ingrid Kristiansen**

commercial circus, how you tackle the media are very important.

I believe that a workout consists of two phases, the work phase and the rest phase. Both have the same importance, and the balance of the two gives the final result of the workout.

My body always knows best how a workout should be done, and it will tell me if I am willing to listen. This is something most people in the Western world have forgotten.

People in our part of the world are normally externally controlled. They do things because they see and read what other people do—most often the so-called "idols."

The sports magazines always serve their wonder program of how to be in top shape in six weeks, and some people are stupid enough to follow it. The Western world is therefore very trend-oriented, where most of us blindly follow the pack like sheep. This results in collectively doing the same things, and very often the wrong things.

We clearly see that African athletes still are internally controlled; they use their intuition. If they are tired, they rest and have no guilt feelings about it. They have no idea about all the wonder programs needed to be the best—and as a result they are the best.

Because of what I said above, I hesitate to give an example of my typical training.

# DOUG KURTIS

*Recovery rates slow down with age, and each marathon eats away further at the ability to bounce back. So reads the published advice, and for most runners it might apply. But not to Kurtis. Now in his 40s, he still competes at marathon-a-month pace. His 76 sub-2:20s, 12 races below that time in a single year and 38 career victories (through mid-1995) are all the highest counts ever recorded.*

## ❏ DOUGLAS T. KURTIS

Northville, Michigan. Born March 12th, 1952, in Detroit, Michigan. 5'8", 130 pounds. Married, two children. Occupation: systems analyst, runner. Began racing in 1968. Runs for Nike and Redford Roadrunners. Self-coached.

## ❏ BEST TIMES

Mile, 4:15; 8-K, 23:25; 10-K, 29:44; 10 miles, 48:30; half-marathon, 1:04:51; marathon, 2:13:34.

## ❏ TRAINING PLAN

Consistency, consistency! My runs in Northville are fun, scenic, hilly. I train alone (or start out with my wife) most of the time, but prefer training partners to be able to run faster. My marathons are my long runs. "Junk miles" are okay for me; just get the miles in. One speeed workout a week helps.

## ❏ SAMPLE WEEK

Of 89 miles.

Sunday—10 miles, 1:12.

Monday—A.M., six miles, 45 minutes. P.M., eight miles, 56

minutes.

Tuesday—A.M., six miles, 44 minutes. P.M., two-mile warmup;
8 x 800, 2:26 average, with 200 jog; two-mile warmdown.

Wednesday—A.M., six miles, 44 minutes; P.M., eight miles,
58 minutes.

Thursday—A.M., eight miles, 1:03; P.M., eight miles, 1:01.

Friday—six miles; travel to Charleston, South Carolina.

Saturday—A.M., two-mile warmup; Cooper River Bridge 10-
K in 31:48; P.M., six miles, 48 minutes.

❑ FAVORITE WORKOUT

The 8 x 800 session listed above for Tuesday.

# ANNE MARIE LAUCK

She's the youngest runner in this book. But don't mistake her youth for inexperience. Lauck won the World University Games 10,000 at age 21, and made three straight World Championships 10-K teams by the time she was 26. Lauck ran 2:30:19 in her first marathon finish. It must be exciting to have done so much already, and to have the time to do so much more.

## ❏ ANNE MARIE (LETKO) LAUCK

Marietta, Georgia. Born March 7th, 1969, in Rochester, New York. 5'6½", 105 pounds. Married, no children. Occupation: athlete. Began racing in 1983. Runs for Nike. Coach: Tom Fleming.

## ❏ BEST TIMES

1600, 4:38 (1994); 3000, 9:03 (1991); track 5000, 15:43 (1994); road 5-K, 15:32 (1992); track 10,000, 31:37 (1993); road 10-K, 31:52 (1994); 15-K, 48:43 (1994); half-marathon, 1:10:01 (1994); marathon, 2:30:19 (1994).

## ❏ TRAINING PLAN

Quality over quantity rules. Always make sure to keep up speed through 400-meter repeats (once a week, even in marathon training). I believe in a higher-mileage program. However, I pay close attention to what my body can handle. If a quality workout starts to suffer, then I know to back off on the mileage.

## ❏ SAMPLE WEEK

Of 95 miles, including weight training for upper body on Monday, Wednesday and Saturday.

**Anne Marie Lauck**

Sunday—12-13-miles on hilly, soft-surface trails, 6:15-6:30 pace.

Monday—A.M., eight miles, 6:15-6:30 pace. P.M., five miles, 6:15-6:30 pace.

Tuesday—A.M., seven miles at good clip, 5:50-6:00 pace. P.M., three-mile warmup; 4 x 100 strides; 4 x 2000, usually at 10-K goal pace or slightly faster, with 400 between; two-mile warmdown.

Wednesday—A.M., five miles, 6:30 pace. P.M., five miles, 6:30 pace.

Thursday—10 miles, 6:10-6:30 pace.

Friday—A.M., seven miles, 5:50-6:00 pace. P.M., three-mile warmup and strides; three sets of 4 x 400 with 200 between (400 between sets), first set 67-68, second set 66-67, third set 65-66; two-mile warmdown.

Saturday—A.M., eight miles easy, 6:45-7:00 pace. P.M., five miles easy, 6:45-7:00 pace.

## ❏ FAVORITE WORKOUT

Track session of 3200 under 10 minutes; 400-800 recovery; 1600 under 4:50; 400-600 recovery; 800 under 2:20; 400-600 recovery; 2 x 400 in 65-66 seconds, 400 between. When I attain these times, I know I'm in great shape for a 10-K on the track. Great combination of strength and speed.

# JERRY LAWSON

When he ran a 2:10:27 marathon in 1993—a four-minute
PR and fastest by an American that year—we asked, "Who
is this guy, and where did he come from?" Lawson's was
a classic case of quietly developing for a dozen years into an
"overnight sensation." An NCAA track All-American in
the 10,000 back in 1987, he had run a 28:21 road 10-K two
years before the breakthrough marathon.

❏ **GERALD J. LAWSON**

Daly City, California. Born July 2nd, 1966, in Syracuse, New
York. 6'0", 153 pounds. Occupation: athlete. Single. Began
racing in 1981. Runs for Nike. Self-coached.

❏ **BEST TIMES**

Mile, 4:04 (1994); steeplechase, 9:11 (1992); track 5000, 13:55
(1987); road 5-K, 13:55 (1993); 8-K, 22:59 (1993); track 10,000,
28:44 (1994); road 10-K, 28:21 (1991); 12-K, 35:39 (1992); 15-K,
44:38 (1992); 10 miles, 47:59 (1992); half-marathon, 1:03:45
(1990); 25-K, 1:15:36 (1990); marathon, 2:10:27 (1993).

❏ **TRAINING PLAN**

Mileage base, then stamina, then stength, then speed, then
rest. Try to pick four or five goal races per year.  Race and
train through races until two to four weeks before the goal
race.

❏ **SAMPLE WEEK**

Of 134 miles.

Sunday—20 miles.

Monday—three-mile warmup; 24 x 200 in 32-34 seconds with 30 seconds between; three-mile cooldown.

Tuesday—A.M., seven miles. P.M., 15 miles.

Wednesday—A.M., five miles. P.M., three-mile warmup; 1.5 miles in 6:43, 800 recovery, 1.25 miles in 5:37, 800 recovery, mile in 4:30, 800 recovery, three-quarter mile in 3:21, mile recovery, two-mile in 9:08; three-mile cooldown.

Thursday—A.M., 6.5 miles. P.M., 13.5 miles.

Friday—A.M., seven miles. P.M., 15 miles.

Saturday—A.M., 5.5 miles. P.M., 3.5-mile warmup; 16 x 400 in 60-64 seconds with 200 recovery; three-mile cooldown.

## ❏ FAVORITE WORKOUT

The one on Wednesday above. When I can nail the two-mile at the end, I have a good assessment of my strength.

# JOE LeMAY

*Twenty years ago, Tom Fleming was known as a big, tough, heavy-training athlete. Fleming now coaches in the greater New York City area. His current top male athlete, LeMay reminds the coach of himself: big and strong (Joe is 6'4") and thriving on high mileage (up to 140 a week). LeMay had just improved his 10,000 time to 28:33 when surveyed for this book.*

❏ **JOSEPH B. LeMAY**

Danbury, Connecticut. Born December 5th, 1966, in White Plains, New York. 6'4", 156 pounds. Single. Occupation: computer consultant. Began racing in 1977. Runs for Adidas Running Room. Coach: Tom Fleming.

❏ **BEST TIMES**

5000, 13:44.1 (1993); 10,000, 28:33.61 (1995); 10 miles, 47:25 (1995); 20-K, 1:00:24 (1994); half-marathon, 1:04:03 (1994); marathon, 2:16:56 (1994).

❏ **TRAINING PLAN**

Strength approach—100-mile-plus weeks are typical except for near race time. Once or twice a week on the track. For a marathon, I get up to 140 miles for three weeks, then cut it to 80 for recovery, then back up for another three weeks.

❏ **SAMPLE WEEK**

Of 108 miles.

Sunday—A.M., 14 miles at about 6:20 pace. P.M., easy six-plus miles in 43 minutes.

Monday—A.M., nine miles at 6:30 pace. P.M., five miles at 6:20 pace.

Tuesday—A.M., 2.5- to three-mile warmup; 6 x 800 in 2:12; 2.5- to three-mile warmdown. P.M., five miles at 6:20 pace.

Wednesday—A.M., run to gym, lift and return, nine miles. P.M., five miles at 6:20 pace.

Thursday—A.M., hilly 11 miles at 6:10 pace. P.M., five miles at 6:20 pace.

Friday—A.M., 2.5-mile warmup; 3 x 1200 in 3:30, 3:25, 3:25; 2 x 800 in 2:15; 2.5-mile warmdown. P.M., five miles at 6:30 pace.

Saturday—A.M., nine miles at 6:00 pace. P.M., six miles at 6:20 pace.

❏ FAVORITE WORKOUT

3 x 1200 and 2 x 800 at 65-second 400 pace. Good distance workout, and I've been doing it since 1986, so I know where I am with it.

# PETER MAHER

Distance runners come in sizes small to tall, but the best
of them are uniformly slim. Seeing Maher now, you'd
notice his 6'5" height but would see his leanness as typical.
You couldn't see that he once carried almost 100 additional
pounds. This was during a pause after his first stint as a
runner. Maher came back later, shed the weight and became one of the fastest marathoners in Canadian history.

## ❏ PETER KEVIN MAHER

St. Petersburg, Florida, and Thornhill, Ontario. Born March
30th, 1960, in Ottawa, Ontario. 6'5", 152 pounds. Married, two
children. Occupation: "full-time marathoner." Began racing
in 1969. Runs for Toronto Olympic Club. Coach: Eddy Rapozo.

## ❏ BEST TIMES

1500, 3:55 (1990); 3000, 8:09 (1990); track 5000, 13:50 (1989);
track 10,000, 29:02 (1987 & '90); 15-K, 44:06 (1990); 20-K, 59:18
(1990); half-marathon, 1:02:18 (1991); 25-K, 1:14:28 world best
(1991); 30-K, 1:32:55 (1991); marathon, 2:11:46 (1991).

## ❏ TRAINING PLAN

High mileage to build strength for marathon, up to 140 miles
per week. Including long reps of one and two miles and 400s
to keep efficient, one tempo run, one medium-long run and
one long run each week; the rest "fillers."

## ❏ SAMPLE WEEK

Of 128 miles from July 1995.

Sunday—22 miles, first 13-14 mainly flat followed by eight

miles of hills.

Monday—A.M., 60 minutes easy, 6:10-6:15 pace. P.M., 40 minutes relaxed, 6:00 pace.

Tuesday—A.M., 35 minutes easy. P.M., three-mile warmup; several strides; 2 x 400 in 63 seconds; 6 x mile, averaging 4:34 with 400 recovery; two-mile cooldown.

Wednesday—A.M., two-mile warmup; 40 minutes of steady tempo, 5:10 pace. P.M., two-mile warmup; 10 miles including 10-K in 34:40; two-mile cooldown.

Thursday—A.M., four miles easy. P.M., two-miles warmup; strides; 20 x 400 in 63-64 seconds (last four in 63, 62, 61, 60), one-minute recovery; two-mile cooldown.

Friday—A.M., 10 miles including 10-K in 34:15. P.M., 10 miles, relaxed group run.

Saturday—A.M., two-mile warmup; strides; six miles in 28:56; two-mile cooldown. P.M., six miles easy.

❏ **FAVORITE WORKOUT**

6-8 x 1600 in sub-4:30 with 400 recovery jog. I feel when I can do this on Tuesday after a long run of 20-plus miles on Sunday, I'm very close to ready.

# SHIRLEY MATSON

*Late starts need not lead to slow finishes. Matson didn't really begin racing until she turned 40, yet three years later she ran in the first Women's Olympic Marathon Trial. A decade later, she came within a half-minute of her marathon PR by running 2:50:26. That time, along with a dozen other Matson performances at distances as short as 800 meters, is America's best for women 50 and older.*

## ❏ SHIRLEY MATSON

Moraga, California. Born November 7th, 1940, in Oakland, California. 5'2", 103 pounds. Single. Occupation: home economist. Began racing in 1981 at age 40. Runs for Impalas Club. Self-coached.

## ❏ BEST TIMES

800, 2:25 (1992); 1500, 4:48 (1989); 5-K, 17:27 (1991); 8-K, 28:35 (1986); 10-K, 35:32 (1985); 12-K, 44:34 (1986); 15-K, 54:33 (1991); 10 miles, 59:08 (1991); half-marathon, 1:19:23 (1988); 30-K, 1:59:25 (1988); marathon, 2:50:03 (1984).

## ❏ TRAINING PLAN

I train by the hard-easy principle, according to how I feel. If rested, I run eight to 10 miles hard; if tired, easy pace. I rarely do track work, as I get injured too easily, and would rather use races as my speedwork. However, occasionally I will do "bursts" of a half-mile or mile in my normal runs.

## ❏ SAMPLE WEEK

Here is how I trained before setting an American 50-54 record for the 10-K in 1991. The week's mileage was 62.

Sunday—17-mile trail run at easy pace.

Monday—10½ miles in 1:26:42.

Tuesday—11 miles in 1:20:05, including two miles in 12:20.

Wednesday—11 miles in 1:20:55, including three half-miles in 3:00 each.

Thursday—no running; travel to Orlando, Florida.

Friday—jog two miles.

Saturday—1½-mile warmup, 10-K in 35:57, five-mile cooldown.

❏ **FAVORITE WORKOUT**

Long run of 14½ miles at 6:50 average pace. I feel fit and strong when I can do it.

# GREG MEYER

*The high-water mark in U.S. men's marathoning may have come at Boston in 1983. Three Americans broke 2:10, dozens went under 2:20, and none ran faster than Meyer. It would be 11 years before anyone from this country bettered his 2:09:00 that day. He is one of the few runners in history with both a sub-four-minute mile and a sub-2:10 marathon. His former world road record at 10 miles still stands as a U.S. mark.*

## ❑ GREGORY A. MEYER

Hingham, Massachusetts. Born September 18th, 1955, in Grand Rapids, Michigan. 5'10", 148 pounds. Married, three children. Occupation: marketing manager, Reebok Running. Began racing in 1969. Coaches: Bill Squires, Bob Sevene, Ron Warhurst.

## ❑ BEST TIMES

Mile, 3:59.1 (1978); track 5000, 13:33 (1983); 8-K, 22:45 (1982); track 10,000, 27:53 (1983); 15-K, 43:07 (1983); 10 miles, 46:13 (1983); 20-K, 58:24 (1982); 25-K, 1:14:29 (1979); marathon, 2:09:00 (1983).

## ❑ TRAINING PLAN

Key element has always been strength combined with speed: hard tempo runs, hill repeats and long track workouts.

## ❑ SAMPLE WEEK

Of 125 to 135 miles.

Sunday—20-mile fartlek, averaging 5:15 pace.

Monday—A.M., 10 miles easy. P.M., eight miles easy.

**Greg Meyer (No. 1), among the leaders in the
1984 Olympic Trials marathon.**

Tuesday—A.M., 10 miles including 8 x hill hard. P.M., 6-8 miles easy.

Wednesday—A.M., 15 miles steady. P.M., 5-6 miles easy.

Thursday—A.M., 5-6 miles easy. P.M., 4-6 miles of intervals on track.

Friday—8-10 miles easy.

Saturday—tempo run or race used as training, not a goal race.

## ❏ FAVORITE WORKOUT

Hill repeats, because I could do them alone or with people, and always got a lot from them.

# LORRAINE MOLLER

> No one has compiled a marathon career like hers in terms of quality over time. Nobody, woman or man, comes close. In 1980, New Zealander Moller won the first of her three Avon world titles. . . in 1984, she placed fifth in the Olympics. . . in 1992, she collected a Olympic bronze medal at age 37. Moller's career spans international racing in track and cross country as a junior, and on the roads as a master.

## ❏ LORRAINE MOLLER

Boulder, Colorado. 5'9", 120 pounds. Born June 1st, 1955, in New Zealand. Married, no children. Occupation: athlete. Began racing in 1969. Coach: Dick Quax.

## ❏ BEST TIMES

1500, 4:10.3; mile, 4:32.4; 3000, 8:51.7; track 5000, 15:32.9; road 5-K, 15:23; track 10,000, 32:24; road 10-K, 32:06; 15-K, 49:07; 10 miles, 53:17; 20-K, 1:08:12; marathon, 2:28:17.

## ❏ TRAINING PLAN

I take a block of time, say six months, that culminates in a marathon. My training is a pyramid approach, beginning with a buildup of endurance running to increase aerobic capacity, adding aerobic-threshold runs, anaerobic work and racing, and finally a taper before the big event.

## ❏ SAMPLE WEEK

Of 102 miles from summer 1995.

Sunday—long run of two hours and 30 minutes, 20-21 miles.

Monday—A.M., 40 minutes easy, about six miles. P.M., one

**Lorraine Moller**

hour easy, about nine miles.

Tuesday—A.M., 40 minutes easy, about six miles. P.M., 20 minutes easy, 20 minutes hard, 20 minutes easy; about 9½ miles.

Wednesday—one hour and 30 minutes at 8500 feet altitude; about 12 miles.

Thursday—A.M., 40 minutes easy, about six miles. P.M., three-mile warmup; 6 x 1000 in 3:16 average with 600 recovery; three-mile warmdown; total 12 miles.

Friday—A.M., 40 minutes easy, about six miles. P.M., 40 minutes easy, including 6 x 100 strides; about six miles.

Saturday—three-mile warmup; 5-K steady-state run on road in 16:32; four-mile warmdown; total 10 miles.

## ❏ FAVORITE WORKOUT

I enjoy them all, because in the context of my goal they are getting me to where I want to go. Also I like the variety of different sessions.

# KENNY MOORE

*From tragedy rose his best efforts. Moore was awaiting his 1972 Olympic Marathon when the terrorist killings of Israelis occurred. Though deeply shaken, he ran the race of his life to finish fourth. Sports Illustrated then asked Moore to describe the events in Munich. This wasn't his first published work, but it established him as a writer who could deliver under pressure.*

## ❏ KENNETH C. MOORE

Kailua, Hawaii. Born December 1st, 1943, in Portland, Oregon. 6'10", 148 pounds. Single. Occupation: writer. Began racing in 1958. Ran for Oregon Track Club. Coach: Bill Bowerman.

## ❏ BEST TIMES

Mile, 4:03.2 (1972); two miles, 8:43.4 (1965); 5000, 13:44.0 (1972); track 10,000, 28:47.6 (1970); road 10-K, 28:32 (1973); marathon, 2:11:36 (1970).

## ❏ TRAINING PLAN

Basic cycle of three hard workouts (one long run, one short-interval workout, one long-interval or pace-run workout) followed, taking care to do sufficient easy days after each for FULL recovery. Cycle was longer than a week.

## ❏ SAMPLE WEEK

Run in Norway, during August 1972 while preparing for the Munich Olympics; 96 miles.

Sunday—30 miles in 3:03 over hilly terrain; smooth, largely

unpaved roads.

Monday—A.M., three-mile jog. P.M., three-mile jog, stretching (not much).

Tuesday—A.M., three-mile jog. P.M., three-mile jog, stretching (dip in Sognsvath Lake).

Wednesday—A.M., three-mile jog. P.M., 16 x 300, first 15 in 45 seconds, last in 42, with 100 jog in 60 seconds for recovery; five-mile easy run; 4 x 100 strides at seven-eighths effort.

Thursday—A.M., three-mile jog. P.M., three-mile jog, 20 pullups.

Friday—A.M., three-mile jog. P.M., three-mile jog.

Saturday—A.M., three-mile jog. P.M., 8 x 1200 meters in 3:21 (last one in 3:12) with 400 jog recovery; five-mile easy run; 4 x 100 strides at seven-eighths effort.

❏ **FAVORITE WORKOUT**

"Favorite" and "most valuable" might well be at odds. I loved the 30- to 35-mile runs with all my perverse soul. The most valuable is hard to pick, because ALL the bases (speed, endurance, threshold-building) had to be touched.

# MARK NENOW

Nenow kept his training simple. He ran the same workouts almost every day, put in lots of miles, didn't time his runs, avoided track intervals and raced himself into racing shape. It worked for him. He set a world road 10-K record that lasted for 10 years. It remains America's best, as does his 10,000 on the track, a mark set in 1986.

## ❏ MARCUS JAMES NENOW

Hillsboro, Oregon. Born November 16th, 1957, at Fargo, North Dakota. 5'9", 130 pounds. Single. Occupation: Nike sports marketing. Began racing in 1975. Ran for Todds Road Stumblers, Nike, Puma, Asics. Self-coached.

## ❏ BEST TIMES

Mile, 4:02 (1986); 3000, 7:43 (1989); 5000, 13:18 (1984); track 10,000, 27:20.56 (1986); road 10-K, 27:22 (1984).

## ❏ TRAINING PLAN

Moderate to high miles, 115-plus, at whatever pace felt right (pretty quick most of the time, varied pace, almost fartlek). Thirteen runs per week, with second run usually at night.

## ❏ SAMPLE WEEK

Of 115 or more miles, from the 1980s.

Sunday—18 to 20 miles.

Monday through Saturday—Afternoon, 10-12 miles. Night, 6-7 miles. Sometimes a hill workout, a continuous run up and down (both hard) for 30 minutes or more.

**Mark Nenow (No. 133) at the 1984 Olympic Trials.**

## ❏ FAVORITE WORKOUT

Honestly, I had no favorite or trigger workout. Did mostly the same mileage and courses each day. Raced into shape.

# JOAN NESBIT

> *Few athletes ever get to experience a month like Nesbit had in March 1995. Few had to wait longer for it to arrive, which only sweetened the pleasure. Details appear in the sidebar.*

## ❏ JOAN ELIZABETH NESBIT

Carrboro, North Carolina. Born January 20th, 1962, in Fort Wayne, Indiana. 5'1", 98 pounds. Married, one child. Occupation: mother, coach, runner. Runs for New Balance. Self-coached.

## ❏ BEST TIMES

1500, 4:12 (1992); 3000, 8:51 (1992); 5000, 15:24 (1995); track 10,000, 32:54 (1984); road 10-K, 32:20 (1995).

## ❏ TRAINING PLAN

"Periodization": fall, focus on hills; winter, focus on strength; pre-spring, do 6-8 sets of 5 x 100 sprints once a week; spring, race-pace tempo intervals with gear change (10 x 400 in sets of three, steady-steady-fast); racing season, competition; summer, distance. Within each week, all year round, I do a strength, speed and tempo workout, but change the emphasis during each period.

## ❏ SAMPLE WEEK

Of 45 miles, from fall.

Sunday—A.M., longish recovery run, 55-65 minutes. P.M., optional swim.

Monday—A.M., swim intervals; P.M., 8-10 x 400 hill, quick

**Joan Nesbit in a 1995 race.**

jog down for recovery.

Tuesday—A.M., easy recovery swim; P.M., easy recovery run, 40-50 minutes.

Wednesday—A.M., swim intervals (try to simulate afternoon workout in the pool); P.M., fast tempo intervals, say 7 x 700 around a lake in 2:10-2:15 with 70-second recovery.

Thursday—A.M., easy swim or off; P.M., easy recovery run, 40-50 minutes.

Friday—A.M., easy or off, depending on Thursday; P.M., off, or 20-30-minute jog with strides.

Saturday—race day (5-K/8-K/10-K road or cross country), tempo run or tempo intervals (such as 3 x 2-K on trail with 3:00 recovery).

## ❏ FAVORITE WORKOUT

It depends which period I'm in. In the fall, I love my hills; in the winter, I love my 100s; in the spring, I love my 10 x 400. But most of all, I love RACING.

# ARRIVING LATE

You could feel a little bit sorry for athletes who run the times of their lives before they're old enough to take a legal drink. They haven't spent long enough in the climb to appreciate the peak they've reached.

The longer a runner takes to reach lifetime highs, the better they look. Joan Nesbit waited half her 33 years for the views she now enjoys from the top of the sport.

She arrived there in March 1995—twice within two weeks—as bronze medalist at the World Indoor and sixth-placer at the World Cross Country. No other woman doubled this successfully in such diverse types of running.

Nesbit had always been close enough to this peak to feel a little frustrated at not reaching it. She'd placed as high as fourth in the NCAA 10,000 as far back as 1984 and won the Falmouth Road Race that year. She'd finished second in the TAC 3000 four years later.

In 1992, at her third Olympic Trials, she missed the 3000 team by one place. Her racing career seemed to end there.

She was 30. She wanted to finish her graduate studies (and did, in English literature). She and husband Bill Kerwin wanted to start a family (and did, with daughter Sarah Jane born two years ago). She wanted to coach track (and does, as an assistant at the University of North Carolina).

Racing had to go. But as the hectic years settled down to being merely busy, Nesbit realized, "I can't quit until I quit improving."

Her last year on the track, 1992, had been her best. Why not try for more?

You might think she's trying harder than ever, erasing old frustrations over near-misses. In fact, she attributes her recent successes to a new and more relaxed approach.

Nesbit admits that she once worried too much about her running. Now, she says, "I am motivated by joy."

Going to Europe this spring, she tells writer Kurt Freudenthal, "My main goal was to enjoy the experience. I was not nervous. I think I have finally mastered it."

She elaborates on this theme in a *Track & Field News* article by Jon Hendershott: "With my new attitude, the bigger the meet the better I run. I wish I could have come to this point so much sooner in my career—to realize just how much fun it is simply to run as fast as the body allows."

Nesbit wasn't ready to make this discovery any sooner. She didn't have a young child of her own or young runners to coach. She didn't have them to take her mind off her own running.

"After having Sarah Jane and also starting coaching," she tells Hendershott, "my own running became the least-pressured thing I do. I look forward to all my training sessions—and I really, really look forward to racing. It's all just so much fun."

Nesbit looks forward to her fourth Olympic Trials. She feels few of the old "I gotta do this" pressures. Replacing them is the joyous feeling of "I get to do this!"

Joan Nesbit, at 33, knows exactly where she stands in running and all that it took to get there. And she's loving it more than any kid ever could.

# PETE PFITZINGER

> *"Peter the Peaker," you might call him. No U.S. marathoner could reach top form at the right time better than Pfitzinger. Twice he peaked correctly for Olympic Trials, in 1984 (when he won) and again in '88. Twice he peaked again the same year to lead Americans finishers at the Games.*

## ❏ PETER PFITZINGER

Exeter, New Hampshire. Born August 29th, 1957, in Camden, New Jersey. 5'9", 131 pounds. Married, one child. Occupation: graduate student in exercise physiology. Began racing in 1971. Runs for New Balance. Self-coached.

## ❏ BEST TIMES

8-K, 22:46 (1981); track 10,000, 28:41 (1986); 15-K, 43:37 (1981); half-marathon, 1:03:14 (1986); 30-K, 1:32:51 (1981); 20 miles, 1:40:14 (1981); marathon, 2:11:43 (1984).

## ❏ TRAINING PLAN

Two marathons per year with a 21-week buildup consisting of 120 to 150 miles per week for the first 10 weeks, 100 to 110 for the next eight weeks, and a three-week taper. Would run road races of 8-K to half-marathon during the last 11 weeks for race toughness.

## ❏ SAMPLE WEEK

Of 138 miles from early 1984 in New Zealand.

Sunday—A.M., 22 miles, starting at 6:10 pace, finishing at 5:30 pace; over rolling terrain, working the hills.

Monday—A.M., 11 miles, 6:20 pace. P.M., seven miles, 6:20

**Pete Pfitzinger, savoring his Olympic
Trials marathon win in 1984.**

pace.

Tuesday—A.M., 16 miles, 6:00 pace, on grass, rolling hills.
  P.M., six miles, 6:20 pace.

Wednesday—A.M., 12 miles, 6:00 pace. P.M., seven miles,
  5:45 pace.

Thursday—A.M., 15 miles, 5:45 pace; hilly terrain, working
  the hills. P.M., six miles, 6:20 pace, 10 x 150 strideouts.

Friday—A.M., 12 miles, 6:00 pace. P.M., six miles, 6:20 pace.

Saturday—A.M., 12 miles with four-mile tempo run in 19:30.
  P.M., six miles, 6:20 pace.

## ❏ FAVORITE WORKOUT

The long run over hills. Starting moderately and finishing
hard builds mental and physical toughness for the marathon.
These runs enabled me to run the second half of the marathon
within one minute of the first half and finish strong.

# STEVE PLASENCIA

*What a career! Two Olympic and three World Championships teams in the 10,000. . . U.S.-ranked 10 years in a row in that event. . . then making a fourth straight Worlds team in the marathon, placing 10th in the race. Plasencia turns 40 in 1996, but remains very much in the running for another Olympics.*

## ❏ STEVEN MICHAEL PLASENCIA

Eugene, Oregon. Born October 28th, 1956, in Crystal, Minnesota. 5'10", 145 pounds. Married, one child. Occupation: exercise physiologist. Began racing in 1972. Runs for Asics. Self-coached.

## ❏ BEST TIMES

1500, 3:40.8 (1985); mile, 3:58.3 (1982); 3000, 7:46.66 (1987); track 5000, 13:19.34 (1989); road 5-K, 13:35 (1992); 8-K, 22:40 (1990); track 10,000, 27:45.20 (1990); road 10-K, 28:31 (1993); 12-K, 34:54 (1993); 15-K, 43:49 (1995); 20-K, 1:01:30 (1994); half-marathon, 1:04:30 (1992); marathon, 2:12:51 (1994).

## ❏ TRAINING PLAN

My training is anchored by off-season mileage buildups and a long-range approach to planning. Some emphasis is given to balancing running. If I am running many long races, I make sure I don't completely neglect shorter speedwork. If I am racng only short distances (5-K down), I make sure I work on endurance, too. This balance has prolonged my career.

## ❏ SAMPLE WEEK

Of 95 to 100 miles, from 1993. I run plenty with more mileage and plenty with more intensity, but this represents a good training week.

Sunday—A.M., 65 minutes steady, 6:05-6:10 pace. P.M., 30 minutes easy.

Monday—A.M., one hour and 52 minutes. P.M., no running, light weight workout.

Tuesday—A.M., 35 minutes easy. P.M., 45 minutes, 6:00 pace.

Wednesday—A.M., 37 minutes easy. P.M., three-mile warmup; 8 x 1000 in 2:42-2:47 with 200 jog; first 800 steady, last 200 pushed; 2.5-mile warmdown.

Thursday—A.M., five miles, fastest of 6:20. P.M., 55 minutes with some hills.

Friday—A.M., 45 minutes, easy to steady. P.M., 40 minutes; yoga class for one hour.

Saturday—A.M., 35 minutes easy. P.M., three-mile warmup; 200 in 32 seconds, 100 recovery, 3000 in 8:07, 800 recovery, 800 in 2:05, 200 recovery, 400 in 62 seconds, 100 recovery, 400 in 61, 100 recovery, 400 in 62; 2.5-mile warmdown.

❏ **FAVORITE WORKOUT**

6 x 1600 with 400 recovery. If I run this 10 days prior to a major 10,000 race, I have a pretty good idea of my fitness potential for that competition.

# LISA RAINSBERGER

*There are far worse "curses" than repeatedly missing the Olympic team by one place. That happened to Lisa, of course, in 1984, 1988 and 1992 Marathon Trials. But can you name anyone else who has finished so well, so often? No. And neither can you name more than a half-dozen American women who've ever run faster marathons.*

## ❑ LISA LARSEN RAINSBERGER
(formerly Weidenbach)

Hutchinson, Kansas. Born December 13th, 1961, in Battle Creek, Michigan. 5'10", 128 pounds. Married, no children. Occupation: professional athlete. Began racing in 1981. Runs for New Balance. Coach: Fred Moore.

## ❑ BEST TIMES

3000, 9:06 (1988); track 5000, 15:32 (1989); 8-K, 25:32 (1991); track 10,000, 32:15 (1988); road 10-K, 31:45 (1988); 15-K, 48:28 (1989); 10 miles, 52:32 (1989); half-marathon, 1:10:07 (1990); 30-K, 1:46:20 (1985); marathon, 2:28:15 (1990).

## ❑ TRAINING PLAN

Quality over quantity. I am a larger (and older) runner and tend to break down. So I emphasize getting the most out of doing the least.

## ❑ SAMPLE WEEK

Of 90 miles.

Sunday—20-22 miles, 6:20-6:30 pace.

Monday—A.M., eight miles easy, 6:40-7:00 pace. P.M., four

miles easy, 6:40-7:00 pace; weight training.

Tuesday—12 miles, 6:20-6:30 pace.

Wednesday—12-mile fartlek with three miles at 6:00 pace; six miles with three sets of three minutes hard, three easy, two hard, two easy, one hard, one easy; three miles at 6:00 pace. Entire run is close to marathon race pace.

Thursday—A.M., eight miles easy. P.M., four miles easy; weight training.

Friday—12 miles, 6:20-6:30 pace.

Saturday—track workout: 2.5-mile warmup; two miles, one mile, two miles with two minutes recovery; 2.5-mile cooldown.

Lisa wins the 1985 Cherry Blossom 10 Miler.

## ❏ FAVORITE WORKOUT

The Wednesday fartlek session. It helps me adjust mentally and physically to marathon race pace.

# SUZANNE RAY

> What does having to cope with the darkness and cold of Alaskan winters teach a runner? For Suzanne Ray, it has been "tolerance for the monotony of running thousands of miles on a treadmill from November to April." Ray qualified for the 1992 and '96 Olympic Marathon Trials, and was named the Runner's World and RRCA woman master of the year in 1994.

❏ **SUZANNE MARIE RAY**

Anchorage, Alaska. Born May 4th, 1952, in Anchorage. 5'3", 114 pounds. Married, two children. Occupation: teacher. Began racing in 1974. Adviser: Larry Whitmore.

❏ **BEST TIMES**

5-K, 17:11 (1992); 10-K, 34:54 (1991); 10 miles, 58:00 (1992); half-marathon, 1:15:57 (1993); marathon, 2:40:54 (1991).

❏ **TRAINING PLAN**

My biggest strength is consistency. I have little actual talent, so I need to keep my basic mileage and training program going all year. I average 12 miles a day almost year-round. I run at least two speed workouts (one of these might be a race) and a long run—every week.

❏ **SAMPLE WEEK**

Of 84 miles.

Sunday—18 miles, sub-7:00 pace.

Monday—12 miles with 5 x mile at 5:35 with 400 jog.

Tuesday—12 miles easy.

Wednesday—12 miles easy.

Thursday—12 miles with two sets of 4 x 400, first set in 75-79 seconds, second set in 72-73, with 200 jog.

Friday—12 miles easy.

Saturday—six miles easy as rest for race the next day.

## ❏ FAVORITE WORKOUT

Most fun (while still valuable) is a 10-mile tempo run on bike trails, using pulse monitor to be sure the pace is as desired (usually about six minutes per mile). Most difficult, and one I can only do in my best shape, is one hour on the treadmill, alternating 10 minutes a 5:45 pace with 10 minutes at 6:15 pace.

# PAUL REESE

> *In 1990 at age 73, long retired as a Marine Corps officer and educator, recently recovered from prostate cancer radiation treatments, Reese set out to meet a long-held goal of his. He would run across the United States at the rate of a marathon every day (no rest days). After 124 straight days on the road, with his wife Elaine supporting him in their motorhome, Paul became the oldest man to finish such a crossing. He chronicled it in the book* Ten Million Steps. *Since then, Reese has run across nine more states.*

## ❏ PAUL F. REESE

Auburn, California. Born April 17th, 1917, in Hopland, California. 5'10", 145 pounds. Married, three children. Began racing in 1964 at age 47. Self-coached.

## ❏ BEST TIMES

5-K, 17:49 (age 55); 10-K, 36:22 (age 55); half-marathon, 1:25:44 (age 65); marathon, 2:39:28 (age 54); 50 miles, 6:28:25 (age 52); 100 miles, 17:15:34 (age 54).

## ❏ TRAINING PLAN

In my sunset years, the key elements in my training are to endure and to enjoy. "Endure" means to avoid injuries and hopefully to run every day. "Enjoy" means to have fun. Mainly I endure by doing most of my training at a slow, meditative pace. One way I enjoy is to do weekly speed workouts on the track with a friend of my vintage. Another way I enjoy is through adventures such as running across states.

## ❏ SAMPLE WEEK

This was what I did in my best seven-day period while preparing for my 1990 run across the U.S. The week's mileage totaled 97½:

Day One—16 miles on rolling hills at 12-minute pace.

Day Two—13 miles on flat at 11-minute pace.

Day Three—13 miles on track including mile in 8:28, mile in 8:10, three miles in 26:34, mile in 8:43.

Day Four—13 miles on rolling hills at 12-minute pace.

Day Five—10 miles on flat at 12- to 13-minute pace.

Day Six—13½ miles on track including 440s of 2:13 and 2:12; miles of 8:24, 8:56 and 8:34; three-mile in 26:22, and two-mile in 17:24.

Day Seven—19 miles on hilly course at 12-minute pace.

## ❏ FAVORITE WORKOUT

In my early 70s, I enjoyed running three intervals of three miles with my friend George Billingsley. We ran each three-miler below 21 minutes and walked a 440 between. George also ran across the USA in 1990, part of the way with me.

# BILL RODGERS

---

*What do you say about someone who already has published two books about his own running, and was at work on a third in mid-1995? We can say what Rodgers can't say about himself—that he was and is one of the best ambassadors this sport ever had. His story continues in the sidebar.*

---

## ❏ BILL RODGERS

Sherborn, Massachusetts. Born December 23rd, 1947, in Hartford, Connecticut. 5'8½", 128 pounds. Married, two children. Occupation: athlete, businessman. Began racing in 1963. Runs for Etonic. Self-coached.

## ❏ BEST TIMES

Track 5000, 13:42; track 10,000, 28:04; road 10-K, 28:15 (29:48 as master); track 15,000, 43:39; road 15-K, 43:25; track 20,000, 58:15; road 20-K, 58:42; half-marathon, 1:03:08 (1:05:06 as master); track 25,000, 1:14:12; track 30,000, 1:31:40; road 30-K, 1:29:04; marathon, 2:09:27 (2:18:18 as master).

## ❏ TRAINING PLAN

This information all deals with my current, masters training. I'm a big believer in steady-pace running for the bulk of my training. (As a former marathoner, that had to be my emphasis.) I do hill repeats for five to eight weeks before every race season (spring and fall).

## ❏ SAMPLE WEEK

Of 72 miles from March 1995.

Sunday—12 miles.

Monday—A.M., 6 x 700 on road in 1:53-2:00 with 100 jog; 3 x 350 in 58 seconds. P.M., six miles.

Tuesday—eight miles.

Wednesday— A.M., 10 miles. P.M., five miles.

Thursday—A.M., three miles. P.M., seven miles.

Friday—travel to Mobile, Alabama; four miles very slow.

Saturday—Azalea Trail 10-K, 31:30.

❏ **FAVORITE WORKOUT**

3-4 x 1500 on road with 100-200 jog. Simulates road racing. Necessary for 5-K to half-marathon races. Develops cardiorespiratory, muscular and psychological strength.

**Bill Rodgers**

# RODGERS RETIRED?

May 1993 *Running Commentary*

Don't you believe it when Bill Rodgers says he has run his last marathon. Those were the post-marathon blues talking when he announced that one of the greatest marathon careers in history was finished.

Rodgers said, "Marathoning is one of the ultimate grinds in sport. I've been ground down enough. I don't want to do it anymore."

He proves Frank Shorter's adage that you can't run another marathon until you forget how bad the last one felt. The slowest ones hurt the worst because something has gone wrong and the suffering then lasts longer.

Rodgers still hasn't forgotten his last one, though he ran it more than a year ago. Hot-weather racing has always been a weakness of his, and this marathon in Vietnam was one of the hottest. It dragged out a full hour longer than his fastest race.

But in time he'll forget how bad it felt. He has gotten over worse disappointments.

This wasn't as bad as his first marathon. Twenty years ago, his career at this distance could have ended where it started.

"I now know that it's better to err on the side of caution in your first marathon," he writes in his book *Masters Running and Racing*. "But in my first, I aimed for both a high place and a fast time.

"The marathon had always seemed monumental to me. It should appear that way to anyone who runs it—that is, it should scare you into realizing that you can't go into it unprepared."

He trained okay, but started too fast and drank too little. He dropped out and now calls this "such a miserable experience that I stopped running completely for two months afterward."

He would come back to win Boston, then place only 40th at the Olympics. He would come back from Montreal to win at New York City, then drop out at Boston the next year. He would rebound from that to win three more Bostons and three more New Yorks.

Rodgers probably will eventually realize that he doesn't want his final memory of the marathon to be walking dizzily for the last three miles in Ho Chi Minh City. The best way to forget a bad marathon is to follow it with a good one.

Besides, he's only 45. That's fairly old to be beating the newly minted masters, but it's still young compared to his hero.

He looks to Johnny Kelley as the model for longevity. Kelley, now 85, ran his final Boston Marathon only a year ago.

"Johnny Kelley is my Jim Thorpe," writes Rodgers. "The rest of America may bow to the shrine of Thorpe. But to me Kelley is the greatest American athlete of all time.

"People always ask me if I'm going to do what Johnny Kelley has done. I just can't comprehend running that long. I do want to always be fit and hope that it will always be through running. But I don't think I'll be doing the marathon my whole life."

Yet even while "retiring," he talked of maybe coming back for the 100th Boston (in 1996) and again when he turns 50 (in 1998). He would run it but not race it, as his hero did for decades.

Bill Rodgers could become the Kelley of the next century.

# BOB SCHLAU

*Age catches up everyone eventually. Schlau has just built up a bigger lead on it than most of us do. He is one of the oldest Olympic Marathon Trial qualifiers ever (at 40 in 1988). Few runners his age have gone faster at distances short, long and in between. In his late 40s, he set American age-group records in the track 3000, road 10-K and marathon.*

## ❏ ROBERT M. SCHLAU

Charleston, South Carolina. Born September 28th, 1947, in Des Moines, Iowa. 5'7", 123 pounds. Married, four children. Occupation: financial consultant. Began racing in 1961. Runs for Nike. Self-coached.

## ❏ BEST TIMES

In the 45-49 age group. 3000, 9:01 (1994); 10-K, 31:04 (1994); marathon, 2:17:16 (1984).

## ❏ TRAINING PLAN

Never forget speed; always on track one or two times a week, and strong tempo three- to five-milers. Break the year into marathon season (July to January), and 5-K/10-K season (February to June).

## ❏ SAMPLE WEEK

Of 80 miles in marathon season; 60 miles in speed season.

Sunday—20-22 miles strong, 6:20 pace in marathon season; 15 miles easy, 6:50 pace, in speed season.

Monday—eight miles easy.

Tuesday—5 x mile in 4:56 in marathon season; 6 x 800, 2:23, in speed season.

Wednesday—9-10 miles including 10 pickups in marathon season; eight miles in speed season.

Thursday—eight miles easy.

Friday—eight miles easy.

Saturday—2 x three miles in 15:30 in marathon season; single three-mile, 15:10, in speed season.

## ❏ FAVORITE WORKOUT

There are two: (1) three miles on track, accelerate 5:06, 5:02, 5:00; (2) mile in 4:55, 4 x 400 in 71 seconds, 1200 in 3:38, 4 x 300 in 51 seconds, 800 in 2:23, 4 x 200 in 34 seconds, 400 in 69 seconds, 4 x 100.

# FRANK SHORTER

He might not have "invented" running in the U.S., as
some writers have suggested. But Shorter's victory in the
1972 Olympic Marathon surely caused the sport to boom
sooner and louder than it would have gone off otherwise.
The sidebar introduces the post-boom Shorter.

## ❏ FRANK SHORTER

Boulder, Colorado. Born October 31st, 1947, in Munich, Germany. 5'10½", 135 pounds. Married. Occupation: attorney, businessman. Began racing in 1963. Coach: Bob Giegengack, 1965-69, self-coached since.

## ❏ BEST TIMES

Mile, 4:02.6 (1975); 3000, 7:51 (1975); two miles, 8:26 (1970); three miles, 12:52 (1974); track 10,000, 27:46 (1975); marathon, 2:10:30 (1972).

## ❏ TRAINING PLAN

Two interval sessions per week; no more than 5-K total distance run (e.g., 12 x 400); always faster than 5-K race pace; longest interval one mile at sea level, three-fourths-mile at altitude. All other runs easy. Eighty to 140 miles total.

## ❏ SAMPLE WEEK

Sunday—two-hour run.

Monday—easy.

Tuesday—intervals.

Wednesday—easy.

Thursday—intervals.

**Frank Shorter at a Miami race in 1994.**

Friday—easy.

Saturday—easy or race.

## ❏ FAVORITE WORKOUT

12 x 400 with minimum rest interval.

# AMONG FRIENDS

Frank Shorter first sat down to dinner with me in 1971. He'd become a marathoner that day at the National Championship race in Eugene.

Shorter didn't eat anything. He couldn't. His first marathon had so upset him that he turned green at the sight of food.

Frank showed me that night what I was just starting to realize at the time. I was a hero-worshipper who hadn't yet seen many heroes up close. I held them in awe and imagined they were made of different stuff than I was.

Seeing him this way demonstrated that faster and slower runners are really only divided by speed. We're much more alike than different.

The stars get sick, too. They get hurt. They get tired and bored and worried. They need help from their friends.

Seventeen years passed between the first and second meals with Shorter. The recent one reminded me again that, appearances to the contrary, Frank is still one of us.

We were in Charleston, West Virginia, for the 15-mile Distance Run. We went to a country club for a stand-up buffet dinner.

Frank exchanged small talk with the sponsors and officials during the cocktail hour. But when it came time to eat, they left to find their friends. The most famous guest took his meal alone.

Shorter is, in a way, a victim of his fame. As Olympic marathon champion, NBC-TV track analyst, torchbearer on opening day of the Seoul Games and spiritual leader of the U.S. Running Boom, he's held in greater awe than ever.

His manner makes him appear unapproachable. His prep school and Ivy League roots combine with his natural reserve to give the impression that he is cool and aloof.

Frank is treated as royalty, to be admired only from a distance. Runners are still shy about walking up to him and talking about what they have in common.

Shorter knows this. He now tries to put people at ease, and as he does a friendly side of him shines through the regal bearing.

He approached me in Charleston to start a conversation. That had never happened before.

He complimented me on something or other, and asked about my son who was on this trip. He spoke of plans to visit his early home in Ward Hollow, West Virginia, where his father had worked as a coal mine doctor.

We talked about my recent article on the 1972 Olympic team. Most of his teammates from that year are still active in the sport.

"We had something then that's missing now," said Shorter. "We trained together. We helped each other. We were friends."

Shorter had intentionally tied for first place with Jack Bacheler in track races as far back as 1970, when they started training together in Florida. Shorter and Kenny Moore had shared first place at the '72 Olympic Marathon Trial.

Shorter, Bacheler and Jeff Galloway had trained as a team at altitude for the Munich Games. Shorter had agreed to share the pace in some of Steve Prefontaine's record attempts.

"You don't see that anymore," Frank said. "Maybe the Mormons in Utah [Olympians Ed Eyestone, Henry Marsh and Doug Padilla] do it to a degree. But otherwise, it's basically every man for himself."

Before leaving for Charleston, I'd read a newspaper article about Shorter and then thrown it away. It had good quotes from him, but they didn't relate to anything I planned to write at the time.

After Charleston, they related perfectly to our talk there, and I rescued them from the trash basket. Bill Higgins of the *Cape Cod Times* asked Shorter to assess his role in leading U.S. running to where it is now.

"I understand my part in all of it," said Frank, "and I respect that I have an image. But what's important to me is that I don't try to be someone I'm not." He is not untouchable.

"I want those around me who matter—my family and a few close friends--to appreciate me for who I am. The recognition is nice, but that's not why I do what I do." He does it for most of the reasons we all do.

(Shorter's family has grown since this story first appeared. He and his second wife have six children between them.)

# TAMMY SLUSSER

> *Slusser isn't a pure marathoner. No one as fast as she is can afford to neglect shorter races. But she still shows uncommon devotion to the event—as well as to the international travel it provides. Between 1993 and '95, she ran on the U.S. World Cup team and won four marathons in as many different countries.*

## ❏ TAMARA SLUSSER

Monroeville, Pennsylvania. Born April 25th, 1965, in Pittsburgh, Pennsylvania. 5'2", 109 pounds. Married, no children. Occupation: runner, bank teller. Began racing in 1979. Runs for Team Etonic. Self-coached.

## ❏ BEST TIMES

5-K, 16:30 (1985); 10-K, 33:32 (1985); 15-K, 51:40 (1990); half-marathon, 1:13:43 (1985); marathon, 2:37:14 (1994).

## ❏ TRAINING PLAN

During February through October, I try to do track workouts twice during the week, and either a race or tempo run on the weekend. In the winter, I'll substitute tempo runs on the treadmill for the track sessions.

## ❏ SAMPLE WEEK

Of 65 to 75 miles.

Sunday—10 miles if a regular week, 20 miles if training for a marathon.

Monday—10 miles.

Tuesday—three-mile warmup; 7 x 800 in 2:35-2:45; three-mile

warmdown; 11 miles total.

Wednesday—8-10 miles, easy.

Thursday—three-mile warmup; 10 x 200 in 34-36 seconds; three-mile warmdown; eight miles total.

Friday—easy four miles before race.

Saturday—race; usually 15 miles total, including two-mile warmup and long warmdown.

❑ FAVORITE WORKOUT

Tuesday track intervals: 7 x 800, 12 x 400, 4 x mile, or 800-1200-mile-1200-800.

# JOY SMITH

*Wearing the national uniform means a lot to Joy Smith, an Air Force Academy graduate. She also belongs to an exclusive club—the women who've worn the U.S. colors in Olympic and World Championships Marathons. This group numbered only about a dozen when she joined at the 1991 Worlds. The next year, Smith came within three places of going to the Barcelona Olympics.*

## ❑ JOY MEYEN SMITH

Sugar Land, Texas. Born January 5th, 1962, in Des Moines, Iowa. 5'5", 110 pounds. Married, no children. Occupation: account executive. Runs for Nike. Self-coached.

## ❑ BEST TIMES

5-K, 16:15; 8-K, 26:51; 10-K, 32:08; 12-K, 41:44; 15-K, 51:00; half-marathon, 1:11:43; marathon, 2:34:20.

## ❑ TRAINING PLAN

I came from a middle-distance (800/1500) background, so I feel comfortable on the track. Therefore, I usually place two track sessions (short interval and long interval) within a seven-day period. High mileage (80 or more miles weekly) is incorporated only during marathon buildup. Long run of 12-plus miles is a weekly staple.

## ❑ SAMPLE WEEK

Of 85.5 miles, plus water running.

Sunday—12 miles easy.

Monday—A.M., six miles easy; P.M., two-mile warmup; 6 x

mile with 30 seconds recovery; two-mile cooldown; 10 miles total.

Tuesday—A.M., water running, 40 minutes. P.M., tempo run: two miles, 6:00 pace; mile, 5:30; two miles, 6:00 pace; mile, 5:37; two-miles, 6:00 pace; three miles easy; 11 miles total.

Wednesday—A.M., water running, 40 minutes. P.M., two-mile warmup; 6 x 800 with three minutes recovery; two-mile cooldown; seven miles total.

Thursday—A.M., 12 miles easy. P.M., water running, 40 minutes.

Friday—A.M., six miles easy. P.M., 4.5 miles easy.

Saturday—A.M., 17 miles. P.M., water running, 30 minutes.

❏ **FAVORITE WORKOUT**

Before a marathon, 6 x mile with one minute or 30 seconds recovery. This workout requires concentration and mental as well as physical stamina, which is important in the marathon. Due to the volume, I do this workout only once leading up to the marathon.

# KEN SPARKS

*Quality, versatility, longevity. Sparks has enjoyed them all. In the 1970s, he was one of America's finest half-milers. Later, he became one of the world's best masters milers—and marathoners. His times after age 45 range from a 4:17 mile (a world record for that age-group) to a 2:28 marathon. An exercise physiologist by profession, Sparks does all of his speedwork on a treadmill.*

## ❏ KEN SPARKS

Chagrin Falls, Ohio. Born January 25th, 1945, in Indianapolis, Indiana. 5'9½", 142 pounds. Married, two children. Occupation: exercise physiologist. Runs for Etonic. Self-coached.

## ❏ BEST TIMES

880 yards, 1:47.1 (1973); mile, 4:03.6 (1974); two miles, 9:03.6 (1974); track 10,000, 31:46 (1973); 10 miles, 53:19 (1971); marathon, 2:28:36 (1990).

## ❏ TRAINING PLAN

All of this is what I do now; it was different 20 years ago. I train consistently year-round, 60 to 70 miles per week, including tempo runs and speed. Keys: consistency, intensity and run for fun.

## ❏ SAMPLE WEEK

Of 68 miles.

Sunday—A.M., four miles. P.M. (on treadmill), two-mile warmup; 8 x 440 in 64 seconds with one minute rest between; two-mile cooldown. 10.5 miles for day.

Monday—A.M., 5.5 miles. P.M., five miles. Both runs at 6:00-6:15 pace; 10.5 miles for day.

Tuesday—A.M., six miles. P.M., four miles. Both runs at 6:00-6:15 pace; 10 miles for day.

Wednesday—seven miles, 6:15 pace.

Thursday—A.M., 7.5 miles, 6:15 pace. P.M., four miles, 6:00 pace. 11.5 miles for day.

Friday—7.5 miles.

Saturday—A.M., six miles, easy pace. P.M. (on treadmill), two-mile warmup; 2 x 440, 4 x 330, 6 x 220, all at 64-second quarter-mile pace, one minute rest between; one-mile warmdown. 11 miles for day.

## ❏ FAVORITE WORKOUT

8 x 440 with short rest. Keeps speed and gives me feeling of racing the mile—especially the last part of a race.

# JUDI ST. HILAIRE

*Road racing wrecks the speed, robs the legs of their bounce, works at cross-purposes with track ambitions? It sometimes happens, but St. Hilaire was immune. She ran the roads for 10 years before doing her best track racing—making the finals of the 1991 World Championships 3000 and the Barcelona Olympic 10,000. Track didn't hurt St. Hilaire on the roads, either, as she led the U.S. rankings there in 1993.*

❏ **JUDI ST. HILAIRE**

Somerset, Massachusetts. Born September 5th, 1959, in St. Johnsbury, Vermont. 5'8", 115 pounds. Married, no children. Occupation: dental hygienist. Began racing in 1983. Runs for Nike. Coach: John Doherty.

❏ **BEST TIMES**

3000, 8:44 (1991); road 5-K, 15:15 (1993); 8-K, 25:09 (1992); track 10,000, 31:38 (1992); 15-K, 49:00 (1989); 10 miles, 52:27 (1993); half-marathon, 1:10:54 (1983).

❏ **TRAINING PLAN**

Stress quality more than quantity, except during winter months (December to February) when speedwork is limited by weather. Use this time to rebuild base (75 to 90 miles per week).

❏ **SAMPLE WEEK**

Of 70 to 80 miles from February 1993.

Sunday—A.M., four miles on treadmill. Noon, two-mile warmup and strides; Newport, Rhode Island, 5-K in 16:07;

**Judi St.
Hilaire**

three-mile warmdown.

Monday—10 miles easy in 65 minutes.

Tuesday—A.M., nine miles in 57 minutes. P.M., four miles in 25 minutes.

Wednesday—8½ miles in 55 minutes; arm weights (dumbells).

Thursday—five miles and strides.

Friday—five miles easy; travel to Bahamas.

Saturday—A.M., 15 minutes easy. P.M., two-mile warmup; Grand Bahama 5-K in 15:15; three-mile warmdown.

## ❏ FAVORITE WORKOUT

1600 in 4:45, 1200 in 3:35, 800 in 2:18, 400 in 67 seconds with 400 jog recovery between each. Indicator of fitness, done four to five days prior to important race. Not exhausting; a mental boost.

# KATHRINE SWITZER

*You know her best for you-know-what. But she deserves to be remembered more for what came later: her 1974 New York City Marathon victory. . . her 2:51 at Boston the next year (more than an hour faster than she'd run there in 1967). . . and most of all her directing of the Avon Championships that woke up world athletic leaders to the abilities of women.*

## ❑ KATHRINE V. SWITZER

Wellington, New Zealand, and Vienna, Virginia. Born January 5th, 1947, in Amberg, Germany. 5'7", 118 pounds. Married, no children. Occupation: TV sports commentator, sports marketing consultant. Began racing in 1965. Self-coached.

## ❑ BEST TIMES

10-K, 37:30; half-marathon, 1:26:20; marathon, 2:51:33.

## ❑ TRAINING PLAN

I wish I'd known at age 28 what I know now at 48. I'd have made sleep, rest days and less mileage more important. I think I left my best races in training. I'd have had more fun, tried to find training partners (good luck in the 1960s and '70s!) and been less obsessive. But I had good success, I learned to work hard, and I learned the huge joy of becoming GOOD—not an insignificant feeling for a woman who always considered herself a "no-talent." Now, at 48, I love running more, but it doesn't eat me up, and if I miss a day then I don't fret.

## ❑ SAMPLE WEEK

Of 110 miles from prime years.

Sunday—20-26 miles, begin at eight-minute pace, then 7:30, 7:15, 7:00 and finish at 6:30s.

Monday—A.M., six miles easy. P.M., six miles easy.

Tuesday—A.M., six miles easy. P.M., warmup, 20 x 400 in 80-82 seconds, cooldown.

Wednesday—A.M., six miles easy. P.M. 15 miles tempo.

Thursday—A.M., six miles easy. P.M., warmup, 7 x mile in 5:40, cooldown.

Friday—A.M., six miles easy. P.M., 10 miles at 6:30 pace.

Saturday—A.M., six miles easy. P.M., race or time trial.

## ❏ FAVORITE WORKOUT

It always was, and still is, the long Sunday run—I think because essentially a race is first about being able to cover the distance, no matter what, and the long run always gave me physical and mental strength. Later in life, this translated to always being able to last it out in many other circumstances. When I can put some pace to the long run, too, it serves a double purpose of strength and ability to lift at the end. I was always a strong finisher. The long run also was a way of getting into nature (off the track), and at times then—all times now—to let my mind drift and clean out cobwebs.

# STEVE TAYLOR

■ *Many successful runners turn to coaching. (Alberto Salazar comes to mind.) But not many coach during their prime racing years, as Taylor does at Virginia Tech where he leads the men's cross country program. He was named his conference Coach of the Year in 1994, shortly before competing in his second World Cup Marathon. He made the World Championships team in 1991.*

❏ **STEVE TAYLOR**

Newport, Virginia. Born July 10th, 1965. 5'7", 135 pounds. Married. Occupation: cross country coach, professional runner. Self-coached.

❏ **BEST TIMES**

Mile, 4:00.6 (1989); track 5000, 13:45 (1991); four miles, 18:01 (1989); 8-K, 22:30 (1988); track 10,000, 27:59 (1988); 15-K, 43:42 (1989); 10 miles, 47:01 (1989); half-marathon, 1:02:29 (1990); 15 miles, 1:14:30 (1987); marathon, 2:13:56 (1990).

❏ **TRAINING PLAN**

My racing schedule is mainly focused around the winter through early summer (December to May), and the late summer through early fall (July to October). During cross country season, I do not put pressure on myself to race. I focus on getting the Virginia Tech athletes ready to run. I hit 130 miles per week when training hard for a marathon. I work on speed early in my marathon preparation and volume the last five weeks leading up to the marathon race. This has my body ready to roll on raceday. The speed is there, and the feel for doing a lot of volume is fresh in my mind. I have noticed that if I do the volume early (at the beginning of the preparation phase) and speed at the end, my body forgets what it is like to run hard for 26 miles.

## ❏ SAMPLE WEEK

During the volume phase of marathon preparation.

Sunday—A.M., two hours and 50 minutes (This is a critical workout. I start out at 6:00 pace for the first 45 minutes, then work it down to 5:45 for the remainder of the workout.) P.M., 20 minutes easy.

Monday—A.M., 45 minutes easy. P.M., 15-minute warmup; 12 x 400 in 65 seconds with one-minute recovery; 15-minute warmdown.

Tuesday—A.M., 50 minutes easy. P.M., 30 minutes easy.

Wednesday—A.M., two hours and 10 minutes; upbeat run, working down to 5:10 pace for 30 minutes. P.M., 30 minutes easy.

Thursday—A.M., 50 minutes easy. P.M., 50 minutes easy.

Friday—A.M., 45 minutes easy. P.M., 20-minute warmup; 2 x 4 miles, first at 4:55 pace, second at 4:47 pace, with five-minute recovery between; 20-minute warmdown.

Saturday—A.M., 30 minutes easy. P.M., 20 minutes easy.

# ANN TRASON

*The unknowing might think ultrarunners go long because they can't go fast. Trason proves otherwise. She was a high school All-American on the track and can run national-class times in the marathon. But she PREFERS the ultras, and excels in them as few others ever have. The sidebar tells more about her. Ann smashed the world record at the 1995 IAU/IAAF 100k Championships in Holland by almost 9 minutes, running 7:00:47.*

## ❏ ANNE BETHUNE TRASON

Kensington, California. Born August 30th, 1960, in San Francisco, California. 5'4", 105 pounds. Married, no children. Occupation: student (formerly lab technician). Runs for Nike. Adviser: Carl Andersen.

## ❏ BEST TIMES

1500, 4:34; 3000, 9:42; track 10,000, 35:04; Marathon, 2:39; 50-K, 3:20; 50 miles, 5:33; 100-K, 7:00:47; 12 hours, 92 miles; 100 miles, 13:47; 24 hours, 143 miles.

## ❏ TRAINING PLAN

There are four keys: (1) Enjoyment. I like training in beautiful places. Variation is critical to keeping my running fresh. (2) Consistency. I try to get in a run of 30 to 50 miles once a week throughout the year. (3) Turnover. I try to keep some semblance of foot speed. An up-tempo run or track workout once a week is a necessity to achieve this goal. (4) Listening to my body. I am not afraid to change my schedule or take a day off, if needed.

## ❏ SAMPLE WEEK

Of 116 miles from April 1995.

Sunday—36 miles on Western States 100 course, easy.

Monday—A.M., five miles easy on trails. P.M., weights (upper-body only) and massage.

Tuesday—A.M., five miles easy on trails. P.M., 13 miles on roads, hard tempo run.

Wednesday—A.M., five miles easy on trails. P.M., 15 miles on hilly trails, hard run with group.

Thursday—A.M., five miles easy on trails. P.M., five miles easy on trails; weights.

Friday—A.M., five miles easy on trails. P.M., track workout of 1.5-mile warmup; 3 x mile in 5:10-5:20 with 800 between; mile warmdown.

Saturday—A.M., five miles easy on trails. P.M., 10 miles easy on trails; weights.

## ❏ FAVORITE WORKOUT

The long run. My goal is to work up to running half the distance I am going to race—at the pace I hope to maintain throughout the first half of the race. This is true especially for 100-mile races.

# RACIN' TRASON

As runners who make heroes of other runners, we admire the most those who compete well for a long time under all conditions and at any distance. We reserve the highest pedestals for people who display durability, consistency and versatility.

Think about who best meets those standards. Of American men, Craig Virgin qualifies. He made three Olympic track teams, won two World Cross Country titles and ran a 2:10 marathon between 1976 and '84.

Mary Slaney, Francie Larrieu Smith and Lynn Jennings stand atop the women's list. All three have raced at high levels from their teens into their 30s.

Slaney's American outdoor track records range from 800 to 10,000 meters. She has set indoor marks at the short end of that range and held a road best at the long end.

Larrieu Smith made her first Olympic team as a teenager in the 1500. She might make her last one at 39 in the marathon.

Lynn Jennings stars in all the disciplines: cross country (world champion), indoor track (U.S. 3000 and 5000 record holder), outdoor track (likely to be world-ranked this year) and road (America's fastest 10-K woman).

Yet if we think about sheer range of mileage, none of these runners comes close to a lesser-known woman named Ann Trason. She is typecast as an ultrarunner and has incredible credentials in that branch of the sport.

Trason, a 30-year-old from Oakland, California, has won the Western States 100 the past two summers. Not content with a single 100 this year, she doubled back in August to win the Leadville, Colorado, mountain race.

Last fall, Trason beat all the women AND men in the National Championship 24-hour race while going 143 miles. On the way, she set a world women's 100-mile record of 13:55:02.

For all that, though, she still carried the ultrarunners' stereotype. Standard runners think of them as people who've removed themselves from the rest of the sport. Either they never could run very fast, or all of those slow miles have cost them that ability.

Five years ago, Trason ran a 2:40:55 marathon. She was just getting into ultras then, at age 25—almost a baby at distances which the masters dominate. (Bernd Heinrich was in his 40s when he set several American ultra records, and master Sandra Kiddy is one of the fastest women of any age.)

Trason's name disappeared from the lists of top U.S. marathoners in following years. "See," said believers in the run-long-lose-speed theory, "she can't run fast anymore."

It wasn't that she couldn't. She just didn't—not until this fall.

Trason entered the Portland Marathon in September. And won. And qualified for the Olympic Trial.

After running 2:42:07, she said, "I just wanted to come out and have a good time. This was my speed workout for the week. I usually run a lot longer than this, so I was just warming up."

She probably was the only runner in Portland that day to view a marathon that way. She treated it as other marathoners would a 10-K to 15-K race during the sharpening phase of their training. And no marathon specialist beat her.

(Trason has since broken 2:40 in the marathon, won many more ultras, and earned induction into the Road Runners Club of America Hall of Fame.)

# JOHN TREACY

*Experience isn't a requirement of marathoners—at least not a specific background at this distance. Treacy took the 1984 Olympic silver medal in his FIRST marathon—but only after becoming World Cross Country champion twice. Neither is extensive experience in the marathon a negative for runners who know how to ration those efforts and to recover from them. Treacy PRed four years after his debut, and won the Los Angeles Marathon seven years after medaling in that city.*

## ❏ JOHN TREACY

Dublin, Ireland. Born June 4th, 1957, in Waterford, Ireland. 5'9", 127 pounds. Occupation: runner. Married, four children. Began racing in 1970. Runs for New Balance. Self-coached.

## ❏ BEST TIMES

Mile, 4:00.2 (1985); 3000, 7:45.2 (1980); track 5000, 13:16.81 (1984); track 10,000, 27:47.8 (1980); road 10-K, 27:47 (1985); 15-K, 42:47 (1988); 10 miles, 46:25 (1993); half-marathon, 1:01:00 (1988); marathon, 2:09:15 (1988).

## ❏ TRAINING PLAN

When I was younger, I could train harder. In the 1980s, I would typically have two hard sessions a week. I liked to be on the track year-round. In winter, I would run a fartlek workout and a track workout; in the summer, two track sessions per week. A key to training for me was (and still is) my easy days. I allowed my body to recover fully before I went at it again. I also took a month off after track season. Rest is very important. My training in 1995 is a little easier than in the 1980s.

## ❏ SAMPLE WEEK

Of 100 to 110 miles from 1995.

Monday—20 miles easy, 6:50 pace.

Tuesday—A.M., 10 miles. P.M., five miles.

Wednesday—A.M., 11 miles. P.M., five miles.

Thursday—A.M., eight miles easy. P.M., fartlek or track workout (typical track session: 5 x mile with two-minute recovery).

Friday—A.M., 10 miles. P.M., five miles.

Saturday—A.M., 10 miles. P.M., five miles.

Sunday—easy day, 10 miles.

## ❏ FAVORITE WORKOUT

I like long fartlek sessions with four- to six-minute intervals and short recovery time of about two minutes. Total time of hard running, 30 minutes.

**John Treacy in a 1986 race.**

# MARIA TRUJILLO

■ *It wasn't her fastest race or her stiffest competition. But the 1995 Pan-American Games provided a crowning moment for Trujillo. She won the marathon while representing her country of choice and longest residence, the United States. Earlier she'd run for her country of birth, Mexico, in the inaugural Olympic Marathon for women.*

## ❏ MARIA TRUJILLO

Marina, California. Born October 19th, 1959, in Mexico. 5'3", 110 pounds. Occupation: runner, student. Single. Began racing in 1979. Runs for Nike. Self-coached.

## ❏ BEST TIMES

5-K, 15:51 (1989); 10-K, 32:26 (1990); marathon, 2:28:53 (1990).

## ❏ TRAINING PLAN

I train all year long with some months of light training (30 to 50 miles a week) and some with more miles (80 to 90 a week). When competing, I try to get one speed workout and a race each week.

## ❏ SAMPLE WEEK

Of 60 to 80 miles.

Sunday—10 miles; easy, hilly run at about 7:30 pace in the woods with a group.

Monday—A.M., 30-50 minutes easy on beach or trails. P.M., 8-10 miles on trails with rolling hills.

Tuesday—A.M., 30-40 minutes easy on trails. P.M., 5 x mile at 5:35-5:40.

Wednesday—10 miles at medium pace, about 7:00.

Thursday—A.M., 30-40 minutes easy on trails. P.M., 12 x 400 in 77-78 seconds.

Friday—8-10 miles easy on rolling hills.

Saturday—14-20 miles at 6:30-7:00 pace by the ocean.

## ❑ FAVORITE WORKOUT

Three to four two-mile repeats. When I can keep 5:30 pace, I feel ready for a marathon.

# JOHN TUTTLE

> Tuttle might have made a good run at the Olympic team on the track. He ran an 8:35 steeplechase early and might have gone much faster. Instead he opted rather young to become a marathoner—and went to the Los Angeles Games that way at 25. He now is one of the country's rare four-time qualifiers for the Marathon Trials.

## ❏ JOHN TUTTLE

Douglasville, Georgia. Born October 16th, 1958, in Alfred, New York. 6'0", 146 pounds. Married, two children. Occupation: teacher. Began racing in 1968. Runs for Asics. Self-coached.

## ❏ BEST TIMES

Mile, 4:01.9; steeplechase, 8:35.6; track 5000, 13:45; road 5-K, 13:45; track 10,000, 28:04; marathon, 2:10:51.

## ❏ TRAINING PLAN

Due to summer allergies, I try to run well in late spring, then take a break, then run well for the fall races.

## ❏ SAMPLE WEEK

Sunday—1½ to two hours on trails.

Monday—A.M., 60 minutes at 6:00 pace. P.M., 10 x 400 in 61-65 seconds.

Tuesday—60 minutes.

Wednesday—15 miles fartlek.

Thursday—60 minutes.

Friday—45 minutes easy.

Saturday—A.M., race or hard track workout (5 x mile; or two-mile, mile, 800, 400. P.M., 50 minutes.

## ❏ FAVORITE WORKOUT

On track 10 days before a big race: two-mile, sub-9:00; two-minute recovery; mile, sub-4:25; 1:30 recovery; 800, sub-2:10; one-minute recovery; 400, sub-60 seconds. It takes strength and speed, and lets me know I'm ready to race.

# JOAN ULLYOT

Dr. Ullyot wrote the book on women's running. That was its title, Women's Running, and no book since its publication in 1976 has covered the subject better. Yet if asked what gave her the most satisfation in the sport, she wouldn't say the book but would pick a race. In 1988—at age 48, after 17 years of racing and dozens of marathons, none below 2:50—she broke through to 2:47. She writes, "Put me down as the slowest (in basic speed) runner ever to have run under 2:50. If I can do it, there's hope for everyone."

## ❏ JOAN LAMB ULLYOT

Snowmass Village, Colorado. Born July 1st, 1940, in Chicago, Illinois. 5'10", 130 pounds. Married, two children. Occupation: physician, writer. Began racing in 1971. Runs for West Valley Track Club. Coaches: Ron Daws (1972-78), Arthur Lydiard (1980-89).

## ❏ BEST TIMES

Mile, 5:18 (1987); 5-K, 18:30 (1984); 10-K, 37:18 (1978); marathon, 2:47:40 (1988).

## ❏ TRAINING PLAN

My best results always came from using Arthur Lydiard's programs. I think most runners nowadays don't really appreciate how well he analyzed the various types of training, much less his emphasis on peaking, and how much of an improvement over the year-round baseline one can achieve with this method. When I'm serious about a race, and have the time and motivation to plan ahead, I try to follow this sequence: endurance work (as long as possible); followed by four weeks of hill workouts (twice a week) for strength; then four to six weeks of interval work (also twice weekly) to develop anaerobic capacity, and finally six weeks of sharpening when mileage is reduced and leg-speed developed, along with neuromuscular coordination.

## ❏ SAMPLE WEEK

Of 43 miles, all at altitude of 8000 feet or higher, about a month before setting marathon PR in 1988.

Sunday—no run; hiked with heavy backpack for nearly three hours.

Monday—A.M., four miles, hilly, 33 minutes. P.M., 15-minute warmup; 1½ miles, 9:15; 15-minute cooldown.

Tuesday—A.M., four miles, hilly, 33 minutes. P.M., nine miles, 1:14.

Wednesday—hiked 6½ hours.

Thursday—34-minute uphill warmup; 2½ miles downhill in 15:39; eight-minute cooldown.

Friday—84-minute trail run.

Saturday—4½ miles on track with 8 x 100 sprints (one every 200 meters).

## ❏ FAVORITE WORKOUT

I like short (5-K or less) time trials, at hard effort, once or twice a week, but only repeating the same distance once every two weeks. Thus improvement is obvious, which is very encouraging psychologically.

# PRISCILLA WELCH

When Priscilla Welch first ran a marathon in about 3:26, her husband-coach David told her to aim at going a full hour faster someday. That seemed unlikely at the time, since she was already in her mid-30s and had only recently taken up running after giving up smoking. Priscilla accepted the challenge, however. At almost 40, she made the British Olympic team and placed sixth at Los Angeles. At 42, she completed her one-hour improvement by setting a world masters record of 2:26:51.

## ❏ PRISCILLA WELCH

Longmont, Colorado. Born November 22nd, 1944, in Bedford, England. 5'5", 108 pounds. Married, no children. Occupation: athlete, public speaker. Began racing in 1979. Runs for Nike. Coach: husband David Welch.

## ❏ BEST TIMES

10-K, 31:48 (1985); 15-K, 49:35 (1985); 10 miles, 53:45 (1984); half-marathon, 1:10:46 (1987); marathon, 2:26:51 (1987).

## ❏ TRAINING PLAN

I like a schedule to work from, but do not use it as pure gospel. If it needs readjusting, I'm flexible.

## ❏ SAMPLE WEEK

Of 90 to 95 miles, at altitude. This would be a segment of a marathon training schedule that I used in the 1980s. Now that I'm older, I probably would take extra recovery/rest days.

Sunday—long run of 2½ hours, and possible short second run.

Betty Jenewin

**Priscilla Welch**

Monday—two recovery runs.

Tuesday—track workout, and second short run.

Wednesday—long run of 1½ hours, and possible second short run.

Thursday—track workout, and second short run.

Friday—two recovery runs.

Saturday—race or time trial, and possible second short run.

## ❏ FAVORITE WORKOUT

Long run on a Sunday. Not concerned with distance or heart-rate monitor. Exercises the fat-burning stove!

# JANE WELZEL

■ *How could she have started racing any other way? Welzel was born in Hopkinton, starting point of the Boston Marathon, and Boston was her first road race of any type. Twenty years later, she had run in the World Championships (1993), won a national title (1990), competed in the first three women's Olympic Trials, and survived a car accident (1984) that broke her neck and cost her two years of running.*

❏ **JANE MARIE WELZEL**

Fort Collins, Colorado. Born April 24th, 1955, in Hopkinton, Massachusetts. 5'7", 118 pounds. Single. Occupation: runner. Runs for Moving Comfort. Self-coached.

❏ **BEST TIMES**

Mile, 4:58 (1981); 5-K, 16:38 (1990); 10-K, 33:37 (1988); 15-K, 50:58 (1990); 10 miles, 54:43 (1990); 20-K, 1:09:27 (1992); half-marathon, 1:13:30 (1991); marathon, 2:33:01 (1992).

❏ **TRAINING PLAN**

The key elements in my traning are: (1) long runs, 18 to 24 miles; (2) tempo runs, six to 10 miles; (3) interval workouts, three to six miles of intervals (400 meters to $1\frac{1}{2}$ miles). I do a long run about every 10 days year-round; intervals once a week during racing season; tempo runs in my marathon buildup and winter base training.

❏ **SAMPLE WEEK**

Of 97 miles.

Monday—10 miles in 1:06:30.

Tuesday—A.M., 10 miles in 1:09:02; 2000-yard swim. P.M., five miles in 35:15.

Wednesday—A.M., two sets of mile (recover four minutes), 800 (recover three minutes), 400 (recover 90 seconds), 400 (recover 90 seconds) in 5:27, 2:36, 76 seconds, 75 seconds, 5:25, 2:39, 76, 74. P.M., five miles in 35:05.

Thursday—10 miles in 1:08:47; 2000-yard swim.

Friday—A.M., 10 miles in 1:09:22. P.M., five miles in 35:18.

Saturday—A.M., 2 x two miles in 11:12 and 11:05 with five-minute recovery; 2000-yard swim.

Sunday—22 miles in 2:25.

❑ FAVORITE WORKOUT

Hard long run; I love my long runs. About every third one is at 6:00 to 6:15 pace for $2\frac{1}{2}$ hours. This prepares me mentally for marathons.

# JEANNIE WOKASCH

■ *The word "love" pops up often in her answers to the survey questions. Wokasch loves to run on the beaches of Hawaii. She loves running with her team. Above all, she loves to race. She's known for running marathons on back-to-back weekends, and for finishing of them with a cartwheel at the line. Light-hearted as her approach seems, Wokasch is a 2:40 marathoner.*

❏ **JEANNIE YVONNE WOKASCH**

Honolulu, Hawaii. Born May 15th, 1962, in Sioux Falls, South Dakota. 5'5", 102 pounds. Divorced, two children. Occupation: pre-school teacher, mother. Began racing in 1986. Runs for Farber's Flyers. Coaches: John Farber, Mike Tymn, Arthur Marcos.

❏ **BEST TIMES**

Mile, 5:03; 10-K, 34:45; half-marathon, 1:16:52; marathon, 2:40:21.

❏ **TRAINING PLAN**

I just do it! I run about the same way every day and don't keep track of mileage. I love to race to see where I am, and mostly to get out and meet people.

❏ **SAMPLE WEEK**

Sunday—race if there is one; if not, a long run with pickups from telephone pole to pole.

Monday—A.M., 45-60 minutes. P.M., one hour; weights.

Tuesday—A.M., 45-60 minutes. P.M., one hour with some hills.

Wednesday—A.M., 45-60 minutes. P.M., track workout with my team if possible; if not, a one-hour run.

Thursday—A.M., 45-60 minutes. P.M., one hour, sometimes with hill repeats.

Friday—rest if an important race on Saturday; if not, repeat Monday-Wednesday workouts.

Saturday—race, or rest if racing on Sunday.

❏ **FAVORITE WORKOUT**

I love running on the beach. It is a relaxing run and an escape from the everyday pounding of harder surfaces.

# FINISH LINES

*So there you have them, the training profiles of 80 road racers. Now what? How do you interpret their practices and incorporate them into your own running?*

That task is, admittedly, confusing. For one thing, two runners can reach similar destinations from entirely different directions.

One might swear by high mileage, another by low but fast miles, and yet the two runners might finish in a dead heat. You see all shades of differences in this book.

You also find many different ways of answering the same question. The questionnaire asked only for a "sample week of training."

As noted up front, some runners faithfully reproduced actual diary entries from the period of their best racing, while others chose to list what they do currently. Some picked their single biggest, never-to-be-repeated week; others an ideal training schedule that they rarely match. They wrote their own rules on what to include here.

Then, too, the amount of detail varies widely. You wonder what key pieces might have gone unmentioned.

A few runners even expressed reservations about a book of this type. Hal Higdon and Ingrid Kristiansen still agreed to appear, but only after writing disclaimers.

Higdon, whose career as both a runner and writer spans five decades, filled out his questionnaire. But he also wrote a column of rebuttal to this type of sampling.

"How can I summarize my training habits in the answers to a

half-dozen questions occupying two sides of a single sheet of paper?" Higdon wondered. He equated his workouts over the decades to the "Moveable Feast" of Ernest Hemingway.

"My training is moveable," said Higdon, "because it rarely remains the same. I shift and sway, not from indecision but because my goals change.

"One season, I might be focused on a marathon. Another, my attention might be drawn to the track. Or I may be taking a mental and physical break. Given this philosophy, I found it hard to fulfill the request to offer a typical week of training."

Higdon supplied one anyway. Ingrid Kristiansen didn't.

The triple world record-holder wrote that she wouldn't want to mislead anyone with a sample from her logbook. "I would not like promising girls to blindly do what I have done without more background [training]. What I have done is based on my genetic gifts and on building up gradually for more than 15 years before I was ready for any world records."

She added that "my answer is probably not what you expected. I propose that you reconsider the whole concept and format of the questionnaire."

I didn't. But Kristiansen and Higdon at least prodded me to write this closing explanation on how to read the book.

Keep in mind that you're merely reading a guidebook, not a bible. Realize that it contains only suggestions, not commandments.

Don't try to adopt these schedules as your own, without personal modifications. Remember that even the 80 authors themselves don't always run exactly this way, week after month after year.

Look at each profile as an example of what the runner did, or would like to do, at a certain time. Dissect the schedule into its individual elements. Then fit the best of those pieces, personally modified, into your own training puzzle.